The Seven
Buy-to-Let
Wisdom

TO LET

The Seven Pillars of Buy-to-Let Wisdom
by Ajay Ahuja

Published by
Lawpack Publishing Limited
76–89 Alscot Road
London SE1 3AW

www.lawpack.co.uk

First edition 2004

Exclusion of Liability and Disclaimer

Contents

I dedicate this book to my mother.

Special thanks to Ellie and my family, Anjana, Tom and Rosa.

I would also like to thank David Delaney for our many conversations on property investment, Zach Chaudry on how to make a million, Mandip on how to collect rent on time and Fred on how to collect rent at all! Also thanks to Emily Shah for giving me the idea in the first place, Gavin for his in-depth questioning, Damian for his even more in-depth questioning, and Giles and Nikki for their continued belief.

About the author

Ajay Ahuja is a guru of property investment and author of 13 books on the subject. He is also a chartered accountant, having founded the national accountancy practice Accountants Direct, the first in the UK providing references for the self-employed for mortgaging purposes.

Ajay now owns and controls a buy-to-let property portfolio of more than 100 properties around the UK. He is regularly consulted on issues surrounding the property market and has often appeared on television and in the national press.

Introduction

Buy to let is simple – you buy a property and rent it out, right? Wrong! Successful buy to let is backed by a science that is based on business fundamentals which have been refined over time since the first brick was laid on the first ever investment property. There are seven fundamentals to property investment:

1. Yield

2. Management

3. Gearing

4. Awareness

5. Appreciation

6. Risk

7. Exit

To understand these fundamentals we need to go back, way back, to when the first property deals were taking place.

Yield

A long time ago, when there were no homes people used to live in caves. When the caves became in short supply man had to seek shelter elsewhere so he had to build a home. Now, I imagine there were no building firms in those days, let alone cowboy builders, so man had to build his own home, with his own sweat, and with whatever materials he could find.

Now, there was this one man, Romulus, who had to build his own home. He found out that he was actually quite good at it. In fact, he realised that he was better at building homes than actually hunting and gathering food.

There was another man, Remus, who noticed this as well. Remus used to admire Romulus's home as it was far better than his, but noticed that Romulus's family didn't have much to eat. Remus was good at hunting, but wasn't good at house building so Remus approached Romulus and made him an offer.

'I will hunt and gather 200 deer for you if you build me a home,' he said.

'What will I do with 200 deer? After three months my family and I will have eaten only 12 deer and the rest will go stale,' Romulus replied. 'How about you give me one deer a week for the next four years?'

Remus thought about it and worked out that it wouldn't take him more than an extra two hours per week to meet Romulus's quota, but if he tried to build his own home it would take twice as long and wouldn't be half as good. Remus therefore agreed.

This deal, or something similar, was the first property deal that ever occurred. Romulus evaluated what he would get out of the deal relative to what he had to put in. By investing approximately three months of his time building the house, in return he would receive two deer a week for the next five years, which probably equated to six months' worth of his time. So in this example there is a clear profit element to this transaction of three months. Romulus had to make an estimation, however, as his profit may have been anything from one to five months' worth.

In property investment you have to make an estimation of the profit element and there is no guarantee of what you will get. You can only make an educated guess. The best tool to estimate this is YIELD.

Chapter 1 deals with yield, what it is, why it is important, how to calculate it, what to compare it to and key thresholds that should trigger you to buy.

Management

After Remus's house was built word spread. Many people in the community asked him to build them homes in exchange for resources.

Romulus was building homes as fast as he could physically build them in return for animal skin, metal, wood and tools. Soon Romulus had a well-fed, well-clothed and well-housed family due to his efforts of house building and the 'rent' he was receiving.

Romulus was now earning more than he could use so he decided to use the excess to pay other men to build more homes. Before he knew it Romulus had a fully fledged building company making him enough resources without having to build any homes himself!

Things were not all rosy, however. Some of the people were not keeping to their side of the bargain and Romulus was not getting the full quota from his residents as first agreed. He would get one deer instead of two a week, sometimes none. Romulus realised that if he was to pay his workforce on time and in full, and maintain his family, he would have to take on someone to ensure that all the quotas were paid fully and promptly.

Romulus knew of Conan. He was a strong and well-respected man. Romulus asked him whether he would like to collect the quotas in return for a share of what he collected. Conan agreed. Soon all the quotas were being met in full and on time. Romulus's building company was becoming a strong force and the homes he was building were better due to the amassing of other resources other than just food.

The key to Romulus's continuing success was MANAGEMENT. Romulus realised that not only did he have to calculate what he'd get back, but he also had to make sure that he received it. If you invest money, you need to know that you'll be able to get a return – for real! Theoretical profits can easily become a real loss.

Chapter 2 deals with managing the people surrounding you: you, the bank, the tenant, the letting agent, your employees, the contractors, your solicitor, your mortgage broker, the local authority, the freeholder and managing agent, your accountant and the law.

Gearing

Back to Romulus's story. A few years later came the introduction of money, which got rid of the hassle of doing deals with food, wood, metal, etc. Romulus now wanted to grow bigger. He was growing by simply reinvesting his earnings into wages to build more homes, but Romulus was ambitious and wanted to grow faster. With the emergence of money came the money lenders. Romulus met up with Barclay, a local money lender, who offered to lend him money to enable him to build ten times more homes per month at the cost of one home per month. Romulus agreed to this and soon the land was filled with Romulus's homes.

Romulus's rapid expansion was due to his willingness to borrow. He realised that he would grow a lot quicker if he borrowed. He evaluated the cost of borrowing and found there was a pay off for doing so. It's what's known in the game as GEARING. Gearing is key to business, but even more key to property. With the use of manageable long-term debt, he was able to structure the cashflows so that he could pay the money lender and builders and still make some money on top.

Chapter 3 deals with how gearing increases your return, how to make infinite returns, how to achieve 100 per cent financing, the cost of holding money, and understanding what accountants commonly call the 'opportunity cost' of money and why it is important.

Awareness

Due to the success of Romulus's building company he found that his homes dominated the market. Properties that he had originally built were coming up for sale. The prices being charged seemed quite low in comparison to what he was paying to build them. It was therefore in Romulus's interest to buy these homes and rent them out rather than build them and sell them on! So Romulus did just that!

Romulus was aware of the market enough to change his strategy. You have to be aware of the whole market surrounding you to ensure that you are making the right business decisions. This is what I call AWARENESS.

Chapter 4 shows you how to calculate the real value of a property, how to calculate the bubble element, why the bubble element exists, what to be aware of to avoid properties with a bubble element and predictions on the bubble bursting.

Appreciation

Due to population movements Romulus was seeing certain areas fall, as well as rise, in value due to the increased and decreased demand for properties in that area. Romulus would watch these movements and predict the areas which offered growth to his investment. He realised that if he could buy a property and make a gain without actually having to do anything, it would be easier to make even more money.

APPRECIATION is money for nothing. It's the easiest way to make money. It's the ability to predict the way the market is going. This is very difficult to do as there are many variables involved, but you can make informed predictions over the short, medium and long term.

Chapter 5 shows you how to get capital appreciation without foresight, with foresight and with potential. It explains what negative bubbles are (and how they make you rich) and how to calculate the immediate profit from an extension or loft conversion.

Risk

Romulus had bought in predominantly two areas. This is because he knew the areas well and did not want to cast his net too far. However, there was a terrible flood in one of the areas which wiped out all of his properties in that area. As a result, Romulus's wealth was halved. He had to reduce his living costs to accommodate for this tragedy and his expansion plans were blighted.

Romulus had put all his eggs in two baskets! He did not understand how to mitigate his RISK and did not apply, among others, the principle of diversification, which is the science of spreading your investments over different uncorrelated markets.

Chapter 6 shows you what systematic, leverage and specific risk are, how to eliminate these risks where possible and how to manage what remains.

Exit

Romulus owned many houses, but he was now too old to run and manage them and his offspring showed no interest. He approached Barclay and asked him if he knew anyone who would be interested in purchasing his business. Barclay suggested that he should sell at the right time and get all the right statistics (yields, gross profits, net profits, etc.) in order to attract the right buyer. Six months down the line he approached Barclay again and presented him his business. Barclay found a buyer within three months.

With the money realised, Romulus invested it in Barclay's bank on a long-term deposit account and he earned a healthy interest for him and his family risk free.

With any investment you need to know when to EXIT. It's knowing when to sell and get the most for your investment.

Chapter 7 shows you what is a hotspot, cooling spot, coldspot and warmspot and why you should sell only in a cooling spot.

Now we know the seven most important factors when it comes to property investment, let's get into the detail. Remember that these factors are not sequential, but instead all of them must be understood and applied at the same time in order for you to get the most out of your investment. You need to think about all of them as a whole to ensure your success.

Note: This book does **not** tell you how to do buy to let. You will not find out about the nitty-gritty of renting property or buy-to-let mortgages, such as the types of tenancy agreements or discount tracker mortgages. This book is for the investor who's already taken the plunge and is in the property game. *The Seven Pillars of Buy-to-Let Wisdom* will prompt you to think about the wider aspects of buy to let, the variables involved and how to understand and exploit them.

CHAPTER 1

Yield

The first question of any professional property investor when considering a purchase is: what is the yield? This should only ever be the starting point. If the yield is good, then go for it. If it's not, then forget it! However, first we need to know what yield is and also what is a good yield. Yield in its purest form is:

what you get out relative to what you put in

So to calculate yield you simply divide what you get out by what you put in and express it as a percentage. In mathematical terms, this is:

$$\frac{\text{What you get out} \times 100}{\text{What you put in}}$$

What you get out

So what do you get out from property? The answer is RENT! But it's not as simple as that. Do you consider the rent received, the rent received less mortgage costs or the amount of cash you receive after all the expenses including tax have been deducted? Do you include capital growth? Do you consider it on a weekly, monthly or annual basis? The key outputs you should only ever be interested in if you are considering purchasing a property are as follows:

Cash Buyer
A buyer who is using only his own savings to purchase the property and not borrowing any funds at all.
Output

- **Annual Rent**

  This is the amount you expect to receive from your tenant for the use of the property only. Don't include any payments from your tenant that are considered expenses, such as water rates or Council Tax, if you do include this in your rent. Calculate it on an annual basis as returns are always calculated annually (its industry standard). Assume a full year with no void periods (void periods are dealt with below).

- **Annual Rent minus Expenses**

  This is what you expect to receive back into your hand before tax (this is the annual rent less the annual expenses). Typical expenses will be:

  - **Service charge and ground rent** – If you rent out a flat, you are responsible for all the service charge and ground rent due. These are the costs to maintain the block and to keep the freeholder happy! These expenses can never be the responsibility of your tenant as non-payment can result in the loss of your flat due to it being leasehold. These costs need to be considered before you buy a flat as some service charges can be extortionate.

  - **Insurances** – You need buildings insurance to cover the property against damage or vandalism. Some areas are expensive to insure so try to get an idea of insurance premiums for the area before buying so you can see how much they will affect the overall output. You may want rent guarantees and maintenance insurance, so these premiums will also have to be accounted for.

  - **Letting agent's fees** – You may want to use a letting agent as you have a full-time job or you simply don't want to deal with the hassle of renting out the property. The cost can vary widely – letting agents can charge anything between seven per cent and 17 per cent! Get an idea of what the charge will be first as it will be applied to the rent and will hit the top line.

Cash Buyer

- **Repairs** – With repairs you are in the hands of the gods as you can only estimate what the costs will be! This expense alone can make the difference between making a profit or a loss. Over the long term repairs even out through the life of the property, but if you get hit for large repair bills early on, it can leave you out of pocket for a while.

- **Void periods and bad debts** – If you are investing in a high-demand area, then voids will be minimal, but it's always good practice to assume one month to be prudent. I invest in medium-demand areas and I assume two months for some areas. Also, do remember that sometimes tenants don't pay at all, so the non-payment of rent is as good as a void. I charge one month for this possible inconvenience as standard. In total I charge three months' worth of rent to this expense, which is equivalent to 25 per cent of the annual rent.

- **Administration costs** – There will be letters, tenancy agreements, postage and other office costs involved with running a property which need to be estimated. The more properties you have the less the overall cost will be as the cost is split between the properties.

- **Other costs** – This will be specific to the property. If you are considering buying a flat in Chelsea, for example, then your marketing costs may be high as you may need to advertise in *The Times* and produce a glossy brochure. However, if you're buying a small bedsit up North, then only minimal costs for advertising will be needed, but extra security costs for the property during void periods will have to be budgeted for.

It's good to calculate this output as it will determine whether it's a good investment. If the output is not what you expected, then you can walk away from the deal. If it meets your expectation or even surpasses it, then it's worth considering. This output is commonly called the 'expected net profit of an investment' and hopefully this figure should be positive!

- **Annual Rent minus Expenses minus Tax**

This is another important output. This is what you expect to get back into your hand after everything – including tax. Things to

Cash Buyer

consider when taking into account the amount of tax you'll have to pay are:

- **Allowable expenditure** – You have to check that the expenses above are tax deductible. Expenses have to be incurred necessarily, wholly and exclusively to the business for them to be deductible. If they're not, then they will have to be added back when calculating your tax liability, which will result in a higher tax charge.

- **Allowable reliefs** – There are certain reliefs available to you (e.g. wear and tear allowance and capital allowances) which the Inland Revenue allow you to apply to the profit. Even though these are not out-of-pocket expenses (i.e. no money has passed hands), you can still claim these reliefs in order to lower your overall profit, thus reducing your tax charge.

- **Basic- or higher-rate taxpayer** – If you are a higher-rate taxpayer, you are taxed at 40 per cent (compared to 20 per cent for a basic-rate taxpayer). This means that you receive less of the profit. Therefore it may be more beneficial for you to invest in other more tax-efficient investments geared towards higher-rate taxpayers.

  Tax-free investments benefit the higher-rate taxpayers the most. Tax-free investments, such as ISAs and Private Pensions, are out there as alternatives to property investment. You have to look at the yields from these investments and compare them to property. I can tell you now that property yields way in excess of any other of these investments, but ultimately it's up to you where you invest!

- **(Annual Rent minus Expenses) + Annual Capital Growth**

  This is the expected net profit before tax plus capital growth for the year. Not only do you receive a rental profit, but hopefully there should be an appreciation of your property. There are many investors who invest in property solely for the growth. They are not concerned with making a rental profit (sometimes they are happy to make a rental loss!), but they want to make an above average gain on their initial investment. Annual Capital Growth (ACG) can be determined by:

Cash Buyer

Current Market Value after 1 year of purchase (CMV1) minus Purchase Price (PP) = Annual Capital Growth (AGC1)

Basically, it's how much your property has gone up by in a year of ownership. For future years, ACG is:

CMVn minus CMVn-1 = ACGn

In simple terms, it's the difference between the value of the property now and one year ago.

Mortgaged Buyer

A buyer who uses his own savings and borrows funds to purchase the property.

Output

- **Annual Rent minus Annual Interest Cost**

  This is the same as Annual Rent above, but the cost of borrowing is deducted. This will be the interest cost applied to the loan. This gives a quick approximation of what you'll get back after you've met the immediate payment of the mortgage as the mortgage payment has to be met without fail.

- **Annual Rent minus Annual Interest Cost minus Other Expenses**

  This is the same as above, but the expenses detailed above are also deducted. This gives an expected profit figure before tax.

- **Annual Rent minus Annual Interest Cost minus Other Expenses minus Tax**

  This is the same as above, but tax is also deducted under the same rules and reasons above.

- **Annual Rent minus Annual Interest Cost minus Other Expenses + Annual Capital Growth**

  This is the same as above, but includes growth calculated as above.

What you get out should only ever be assessed by what you put in. So let's look at what you put in.

What you put in

Well, you can be assured that you'll have to put in some of your hard-earned cash! How much will depend on what you've got and how much you're willing to borrow. There can only ever be two sources for investment – your cash and borrowed cash. Let's look at the following table:

What you Put In	Your Cash	Borrowed Cash
Nil	None	None
Description		
Here you put in nothing! This scenario would occur if you were an employee as an employee never puts any cash into a venture – he only takes it out. The yield of an investment is of less interest to him as the employee is not assessing the risk. He will only be interested in how much money he is going to receive and the possibility of the amount increasing in the future. This situation can be ignored as I am assuming you are an investor. If you were to calculate the yield, it would be infinity as you have put nothing in and got something out!		
The only other way this could occur would be if you took on a financial partner. He would put in his own cash and possibly borrow the rest, but would rely on your expertise to make the investment work. If this is the case, then yield is important and all the calculations below would be relevant and valid.		

What You Put In	Your Cash	Borrowed Cash
Nil	None	Purchase Price (PP) + Acquisition costs = Total cost of investment
Description		
Here you still put in nothing! The difference is that you borrow the whole of the cost of the investment (i.e. the deposit, the mortgage amount, solicitor's costs, arrangement fees and valuation fees). On the surface the yield is again infinity, but because you have borrowed all the money your ability to service the debt will be dependent on the yield, so yield becomes very important. In fact, out of all these		

four classes the yield of the investment is the most important as it has to be compared to the average interest rate you're borrowing at. If the yield is lower than the average rate, then the investment will lose money. See below for further information.

What You Put In	Your Cash	Borrowed Cash
Some	Deposit + Acquisition costs	Purchase Price (PP) minus Deposit = Mortgage

Description

This is the normal way people invest in property. You put in some, but the bank puts in the lion's share. Typical ratios of your money to the bank's money are anywhere from 15:85 to 40:60, so ultimately you want to know what return you expect to get on the money you have invested. This is called 'Return On Capital Employed' (ROCE), 'Capital' being another name for your own personal contribution to the investment.

What You Put In	Your Cash	Borrowed Cash
All	Purchase Price (PP) + Acquisition costs	None

Description

If only! This investor is rich enough to fund the whole purchase price and acquisition costs from his own savings. There are no borrowings. This investor needs to calculate the yield so he can make a direct comparison with other investments.

So to calculate yield, as mentioned before, you simply divide what you get out by what you put in and express it as a percentage:

$$\frac{\text{What you get out} \times 100}{\text{What you put in}}$$

So the magic calculations that need to be computed, based on what you put in and get out detailed above, are:

Cash Buyer

A buyer who is using only his own savings to purchase the property and not borrowing any funds at all.

Gross Yield (GY)

Calculation

$$\frac{\text{Annual rent} \times 100}{\text{Property purchase price} + \text{Acquisition costs}}$$

Why it's a key performance indicator

This is a quick calculation to compute. It can give you a quick idea if the investment is worth pursuing. If you calculate the gross yield to be a meagre two per cent, then you quickly know that it won't be too long before that two per cent yield diminishes to below a 0 per cent yield and you will make a loss. Armed with this calculation you can quickly walk away from an investment or on the flipside get very excited!

Net Yield (NY)

Calculation

$$\frac{(\text{Annual rent minus Expenses}) \times 100}{\text{Property purchase price} + \text{Acquisition costs}}$$

Why it's a key performance indicator

This calculation gives us a figure to compare directly with a bond yield or bank deposit account.

Net Yield After Tax (NYAT)

Calculation

$$\frac{(\text{Annual rent minus Expenses minus Tax}) \times 100}{\text{Property purchase price} + \text{Acquisition costs}}$$

Why it's a key performance indicator

This is the real cashflow you will receive after all deductions, including tax, based on the amount you have invested.

Net Yield Including Capital Growth (NYICG)

Calculation

$$\frac{(\text{Annual rent minus Expenses}) + \text{Annual Capital Growth (ACG)} \times 100}{\text{Property purchase price} + \text{Acquisition costs}}$$

Cash Buyer

Why it's a key performance indicator

This is the return on the investment including any appreciation the property may have experienced in the year. This return can be directly compared to a stock or equity investment on the stock market.

Mortgaged Buyer

A buyer who uses his own savings and borrows funds to purchase the property.

Gross ROCE (GR)

Calculation

$$\frac{(\text{Annual rent minus Annual interest cost}) \times 100}{\text{Deposit} + \text{Acquisition costs}}$$

Why it's a key performance indicator

This is a relatively quick calculation to compute. You can get an idea of the return you will get on the money you have personally invested.

Net ROCE (NR)

Calculation

$$\frac{(\text{Annual rent minus Annual interest cost minus Other expenses}) \times 100}{\text{Deposit} + \text{Acquisition costs}}$$

Why it's a key performance indicator

This calculation will give you the net profit figure for the investment based on the amount you have invested. A true measure of the profitability of the investment.

Net ROCE After Tax (NRAT)

Calculation

$$\frac{(\text{Annual rent minus Annual interest cost minus Other expenses minus Tax}) \times 100}{\text{Deposit} + \text{Acquisition costs}}$$

Why it's a key performance indicator

This is the real cashflow you will receive after all deductions, including tax, based on the amount you have invested.

Mortgaged Buyer	
Net ROCE Including Capital Growth (NRICG)	
Calculation	(Annual rent minus Annual interest cost minus Other expenses) + Annual Capital Growth (ACG) x 100
	Deposit + Acquisition costs
Why it's a key performance indicator	
This is the true return on your money after taking into account any appreciation on the property. This return can be directly compared to a stock or equity investment on the stock market.	

An example of how to calculate yield

David buys a property for £100,000 and funds the purchase with £25,000 of his own money and £75,000 of the bank's money. He also pays out £2,000 for acquisition costs from his own savings.

He estimates that he can rent it out for £1,000 per calendar month (pcm). He also estimates the following annual expenses:

Mortgage costs	£4,500
Void periods	£1,500
Service charges and ground rent	£1,000
Repairs	£500
Agent's fees	£1,050
Sundries	£450
Total	**£9,000**

He's a higher-rate taxpayer so his profit gets taxed at 40 per cent. He therefore estimates a tax charge of:

	With Borrowings	Without Borrowings
Rental income	£12,000	£12,000
Expenses	(£9,000)	(£4,500)
Profit	£3,000	£7,500
Tax@40%	£1,200	£3,000

He estimates, based on the previous year's growth, ten per cent growth of the property price (£10,000) after one year of ownership.

So we have all the figures to calculate the yields:

Gross Yield (GY)

Calculation	$$\dfrac{\text{Annual rent x 100}}{\text{Property purchase price + Acquisition costs}}$$
Figures	(12 x £1,000 x 100) / (£100,000 + £2,000)
Result	11.8%

Net Yield (NY)

Calculation	$$\dfrac{\text{(Annual rent minus Expenses) x 100}}{\text{Property purchase price + Acquisition costs}}$$
Figures	(12 x £1,000 minus £4,500) x 100 / (£100,000 + £2,000)
Result	7.4%

Net Yield After Tax (NYAT)

Calculation	$$\dfrac{\text{(Annual rent minus Expenses minus Tax) x 100}}{\text{Property purchase price + Acquisition costs}}$$
Figures	(12 x £1,000 minus £4,500 minus £3,000) x 100 / (£100,000 + £2,000)
Result	4.4%

Net Yield Including Capital Growth (NYICG)

Calculation	$$\dfrac{\text{(Annual rent minus Expenses) + Annual Capital Growth (ACG) x 100}}{\text{Property purchase price + Acquisition costs}}$$
Figures	(12 x £1,000 minus £4,500) + £10,000 x 100 / (£100,000 + £2,000)
Result	17.2%

Gross ROCE (GR)

Calculation	$$\dfrac{\text{(Annual rent minus Annual interest cost) x 100}}{\text{Deposit + Acquisition costs}}$$
Figures	(12 x £1,000 minus £4,500) x 100 / (£25,000 + £2,000)
Result	27.8%

Net ROCE (NR)	
Calculation	$$\frac{(\text{Annual rent minus Annual interest cost minus Other expenses}) \times 100}{\text{Deposit} + \text{Acquisition costs}}$$
Figures	(12 x £1,000 minus £4,500 minus £4,500) x 100 / (£25,000 + £2,000)
Result	11.1%

Net ROCE After Tax (NRAT)	
Calculation	$$\frac{(\text{Annual rent minus Annual interest cost minus Other expenses minus Tax}) \times 100}{\text{Deposit} + \text{Acquisition costs}}$$
Figures	(12 x £1,000 minus £4,500 minus £4,500 minus £1,200) x 100 / (£25,000 + £2,000)
Result	6.7%

Net ROCE Including Capital Growth (NRICG)	
Calculation	$$\frac{(\text{Annual rent minus Annual interest cost minus Other expenses}) + \text{Annual Capital Growth (ACG)} \times 100}{\text{Deposit} + \text{Acquisition costs}}$$
Figures	(12 x £1,000 minus £4,500 minus £4,500) + £10,000 x 100 / (£25,000 + £2,000)
Result	48.1%

So what do we do with these yield calculations? Well, we should compare them with alternative investments (e.g. other non-property and property investments). Once these have been compared, you can make a judgement. A comparison table may look like this:

Gross Yield (GY)	
Result	11.8%
Non-property investments	2.2% – dividend from a stock or equity holding
Another property investment being considered	10.4%

Net Yield (NY)	
Result	7.4%
Non-property investments	4.2% – from a bank
Another property investment being considered	6.5%

Net Yield After Tax (NYAT)	
Result	4.4%
Non-property investments	3.3% – from a bank after tax
Another property investment being considered	4.6%

Net Yield Including Capital Growth (NYICG)	
Result	17.2%
Non-property investments	6.8% – from FTSE Fund
Another property investment being considered	19.3%

Gross ROCE (GR)	
Result	27.8%
Non-property investments	2.2% – dividend from a stock or equity holding
Another property investment being considered	22.6%

Net ROCE (NR)	
Result	11.1%
Non-property investments	4.2% – from a bank
Another property investment being considered	12%

Net ROCE After Tax (NRAT)	
Result	6.7%
Non-property investments	3.3% – from a bank after tax
Another property investment being considered	6.3%

Net ROCE Including Capital Growth (NRICG)	
Result	48.1%
Non-property investments	6.8% – from a FTSE Fund
Another property investment being considered	44%

You have to compare the yields from property with every other investment to be sure that your money cannot be better invested elsewhere and this includes other properties, stocks, bonds, managed funds, banks or other businesses that you can invest in. Be sure to ask the proposer of any investment whether his return is stated before expenses, interest charges, his management charges, tax, capital growth, etc. so you can really compare the investment directly with your proposed property purchase.

Assuming property is your chosen investment then you should set yourself some thresholds. You should set the desired yield figures you wish to meet and then go out and get them. Once you are sure of what you want, then acquiring them will be mere formality – as long as your demands are within reason!

My policy

I adopt the following policy: if gross yield is in excess of 12 per cent and the gross ROCE is in excess of 20 per cent, then BUY! You will have sufficient rental income to cover the mortgage costs and you are being cash efficient with your capital. The thresholds of 12 per cent and 20 per cent are purposely set high to counteract the risk of borrowing (see Chapter 6 – Risk).

If only one of the thresholds is met, then tread carefully. If yield is in excess of 12 per cent but ROCE is below 20 per cent, then you are not borrowing enough to maximise your overall return. This in itself is not a problem if you're not borrowing too much. It is a problem, however, if your borrowing is restricted by the lender due to the lender requiring a high deposit.

If the yield is below 12 per cent but ROCE is in excess of 20 per cent, again tread carefully. As long as the yield is not too far off 12 per cent (I would say ten per cent being the lowest) and the likelihood of voids is minimal (due to the property being near a train station, shops or in a desirable area), then buy – otherwise, stay away.

If none of these thresholds is met, then walk away, no matter how pretty the property is!

Be prudent when using all of the above calculations. Do not overestimate the likely rent achievable, capital gains and estimated profit and do include all the costs associated with buying the property within your acquisition costs.

CHAPTER 2

Management

Management is a very woolly word. What do I mean when I say management? Well, there are 12 parties involved in property investment that have to be managed to ensure that a business is run efficiently and lawfully. In order to grow in any business you have to manage the parties around you. Some businesses grow too large and neglect the management of these parties – I admit to being guilty of this! What eventually happens is that you become too removed from the business to the point where you don't know what is going on. The 12 parties that surround property investment, in order of importance, are:

1. You
2. The bank
3. The tenant
4. The letting agent
5. Your employees
6. The contractors
7. Your solicitor
8. The mortgage broker
9. The local authority
10. The freeholder and managing agent
11. Your accountant
12. The law

Even though you are involved in property investment, which is essentially bricks and mortar, the things you have to manage are people! Property is a people business, so if you don't like dealing with people this may be the wrong industry for you. Let's look at these 12 parties more closely – starting with YOU!

You

Everything starts with you. You have to be a good manager of yourself to begin with and the rest will ultimately follow. But before I start preaching like a self-help guru, let me discuss what you have to manage about yourself that is specific to property:

Manage Your...	How
Space	There's no point thinking you can run a property portfolio from a lever-arch file on top of the TV! You need to designate a place in your house to put a computer, telephone and your files. It could be a section in your living room or it could be a whole room. When I started the property business I lived in one room – that's all I could afford! Yet I had one corner of the room designated as the office with my computer, fax/telephone, printer, stationery and files. Now I have a 300 square feet office at home where I can get away from all distractions, so I can focus on my portfolio and all the administration it brings. Having this space certainly helps to keep your stress levels down.
Time	Property can be a relatively passive way of making money, but it's not completely passive. You need to make time to look at all the administration that ownership brings, all the mortgage deals out there, current property prices and the market in general, even if you only own one property. You have to keep abreast of all matters relating to property if you want to succeed (see Chapter 4 –

Manage Your...	How
	Awareness) and this requires your time. I generally do my administration first thing in the morning so that my mind is free to consider more taxing matters, such as other investments, afterwards. If you hold down a full-time job, then maybe it's time to sacrifice your Saturday mornings for this task. If you do succeed at property investment and leave work, then don't worry, you will get all your Saturday mornings back as every day is a Saturday!
State of mind	You can be sure of one thing – there will be setbacks. Tenants won't pay, repairs will need doing and interest rates will rise! The way you deal with these setbacks will determine whether you sink or swim. If you deem every setback as a catastrophe, you won't last long. However, if you tackle each problem with a positive and clear head, then a logical solution will follow. I am persistent and refuse to allow any investment that I've acquired not to make money. If I did, I would question my own judgement and I wouldn't make any further investments! You have to rely 100 per cent on yourself.
Expectations	Your expectations of others should be reasonable. No-one will ever care for your investment as much as you do as its success does not directly affect his income. So if you instruct an agent to look after your property, don't trust him to have the same urgency as you. Also, don't expect your tenant to treat your property as if it were his own! If you have a sceptical view of all the people surrounding your property investment, it will ensure that you keep on top of things. These people have to earn your trust – don't assume it! As mentioned previously, always rely 100 per cent on yourself – never rely 100 per cent on others.

The bank

There's only one thing the bank is interested in – that you pay the monthly mortgage in full and on time. The only way you can ensure this is by having sufficient funds in your account from where the bank can take payment. Adopt the following practices:

Practice	Description
Keep afloat	Ensure that there are at least three months' worth of monthly mortgage payments in the account. If it comes out of your current account, ensure that there are three months' worth plus whatever else comes out of your bank on a monthly basis. I personally keep six months' worth of mortgage payments in my current account as I am extra-paranoid. I nearly went bankrupt a couple of years ago after forgetting that the bank wanted their money on time! As a result, I hold a large balance because I never want to go through that stress again.
Do whatever it takes	Don't get hung up on where the money comes from to pay the mortgage. If you have to transfer money from your credit card to your current account to meet the payment, then do it! You can always iron out the problems that led to you paying the mortgage with your credit card later. All that matters is that you pay the bank on time and in full.
Bank cash	Bank cash payments regularly. Don't be carrying bundles of cash in your pockets or purse. Mortgage payments are made through the bank, not from your left pocket! This will keep your bank balance healthy and your pockets lighter.
Check balances often	Keep abreast of your bank balance as often as possible. I have Internet banking so I know my bank balance every day. If you don't, you can check your balance from any cash machine if you have a cash card. It is good practice to check your balance daily to see what's coming in as well as going out. This way you will ensure that you can react to shortfalls promptly if they arise.

The tenant

If you have decided to instruct a letting agent, then the management of tenant relations **should** be handled by him. Your job is subsequently to manage your letting agent – see page 25 for further information. If you have bravely opted to manage your tenants yourself, then read on.

It's no good having an investment property without a paying tenant. It's like a shop without any customers. To ensure that you have a paying tenant you have to manage the relationship between you, the landlord and the tenant, in a proper way. Businesses spend fortunes managing their customer relations so you should learn from them. After all, your tenants are your customers. Consider these pointers:

Pointer	Description
He is not your friend	If your friend asks if he can live in one of your properties, say no and make some excuse. We all know the feeling when we've lent a friend £20 on a night out and then we have to ask for the money back – we all hate doing it. There is a good reason why we don't like doing so and it's because money and friends don't mix! Many friends in the past have fallen out over very small amounts of money, let alone a month's rent.
	If your tenant tries to become friendly with you, like inviting you to his Christmas party, always decline. The relationship between landlord and tenant is strictly a business relationship and if this becomes blurred, you are heading for trouble. This does not mean that you have to be overly distant. Remember that you are in business with each other and this is the only reason why you know each other. For the relationship to last, the following simple contract needs to hold – you are supplying a safe property for the tenant to live in and he is paying you the rent on time. Don't complicate matters by drifting into a friendship/business relationship.
Look after him	Having an absent landlord can be very frustrating for tenants; it can result in damage to your property

Pointer	Description
	through your neglect and ultimately the tenant will do the same. If your tenant calls you, answer the phone. If he leaves a message, get back to him. If he doesn't call, call him once in a while to make sure that everything is all right.
	Now I'm not saying respond to his every whim. If he calls you asking for a new toilet because it's dirty (which has happened to me!), politely tell him that even though it's a dirty toilet it still works. Suggest a strong cleaning agent that may rectify the problem, but don't give in to anything more than your contract commits you to. If, however, he has been good at paying and has hardly called you with any problems for a period of over two years or so, then consider it. Is it worth the cost of a new toilet to maintain your relationship with him and lower the risk of losing him? Use your judgement.
Have an agreement	The standard contract that binds a landlord to a tenant is the Assured Shorthold Tenancy Agreement (AST). It's important to have one to start off with and to renew it when it expires. This will set out what is expected from both parties, thus avoiding potential disputes. If there is something particular you want to include in the contract, such as responsibilities for garden maintenance, then do so. It's an idea to talk through the terms with the tenant so that you are both in agreement verbally, as well as in writing.
Stepped credit control	Don't go in 'all guns blazing' if the rent doesn't come in on the due date. Follow a system like the one below:
	One day late – a polite phone reminder
	Three days late – another polite phone reminder
	Seven days late – a polite letter
	14 days late – a letter threatening eviction and court action

Pointer	Description
	21 days late – give him seven days to pay along with a copy of a post-dated eviction notice
	28 days late – hand deliver the eviction notice
	29 days and beyond – commence court proceedings

The letting agent

Choosing the right agent

This is harder than you think! It's not like choosing the right tenant. With a tenant you can credit-check him, get references and take a deposit off him. With an agent it's much harder to get a reliable reference or to check whether he is any good. There are several measures you can take to help you choose the right agent:

Measure	Description
Ask around	Speak to independent parties about the letting agents in the area. If you have an agent in mind, ask specifically about that agent. The estate agent whom you are buying the property from may know of a good one. Ask how long he has been in business and how many properties he manages.
Look around	See which agent's advertising boards are around the most. Biggest is not usually the best, but if you have an agent who is keen to get his name about, it's likely that he will want to do a good job. Visit his offices. Are they in the town centre? Can the tenants get there easily enough to pay their rent? Are there enough staff to handle the calls? When you ring does someone answer? Are his staff smart looking and keen to provide a polished service?
Check his terms and conditions	Are they easy to read and fair? You don't want to instruct an agent and then find out that you have to pay a fortune to de-instruct him. I was once told

Measure	Description
	that I must pay £1,000 to get out of a contract because the agent had found the tenant. I never paid it and he threatened to take me to court. Eventually he went away without payment. If you discover that you've chosen the wrong agent, you want to be able to dispose of him easily.
Speak to the shortlist	Based on the three procedures above, you will quickly get a shortlist of agents. Once you have eliminated the cowboys and the overpriced agents, you can then go and meet the others! The three things you need to ascertain about any agent, no matter what anyone else says, is whether he is:
	1. Knowledgeable
	2. Trustworthy
	3. Hard working
	The only way you are ever going to find this out is through time and time alone.
Choose	If the shortlist is only one, then the choice is easy! Otherwise, you just have to take a chance on the agent whom you feel you get on the best with, who speaks the most knowledgeably and appears to work the hardest.
	Don't get bamboozled by fancy letterheads, state-of-the-art offices or smooth-talking reps. All you should be interested in is getting your rent in full and on time.

If the agent is a member of ARLA, the Association of Residential Lettings Agents, then this should give you some comfort (see the Appendix for their contact details). The real (and only) benefit of choosing an ARLA member is that you are covered against fraud committed by the agent without having to prove who is at fault. However, when selecting an agent, don't rely on this as your only criteria. A letting agency is a people's business and it doesn't matter what professional bodies it is a member of; if it has the wrong people, the job will never be done properly.

Managing your chosen agent

Don't think that once you've handed your property over to an agent it's all sorted, because invariably it's not! You need to keep up to date on what's going on. To manage your agent, you need to act if things don't go to plan.

Problem	Action	Description
The statement arrives late	Ring the agent	A letting agency is usually run by young people. We all know that the majority of young people have other things on their minds! If the support staff are late getting the paperwork to you, then let them know that it's late. As a result, they may prepare your statement before other landlords'.
Payment from the agent arrives late	Ring and/or write to the agent Speak to the tenant	Again, let him know that you know that it's late. Agents holding on to cash really annoy me. It's your money, not theirs! You want the interest that it can earn or, more importantly, the money it can make from further property investments.
Rent is not received on the property	Ring the agent Ring the tenant	You need to know the full answers on this. If the agent simply says that he has written to the tenant, it's not good enough. Has he visited the property? Ask him what HE is going to do about it.
Excessive fees from the agent	Ring and/or write to the agent	If he has added excessive fees to your account and it's not clear where they've come from, get a full justification for the charge. He has to deem the charge reasonable for any costs he's billed for his normal management duties as well as any extras. Estimate the amount of hours he has spent and assume a rate of £15–£25 per hour.

Your employees

If you are in the fortunate position to be able to have employees, then you need to be able to control, motivate and inspire them to run, manage and grow the business. The employees you are likely to have are:

- Rent collector
- Handyman
- Book-keeper
- Secretary
- General manager

There are four management styles and the key to success is to identify with one (namely the last one of the four). Let's look at them:

Management Style Exploitative authoritative
Definition
Management uses fear and threats. Communication is top down with most decisions taken at the top. Superiors and subordinates are distant.
Suitable for Property Investment?
No! We are not operating a sweatshop factory. Let me remind you again that this is a people's business. This includes the people within your business. Dictating your ideas is not the way forward.

Management Style Benevolent authoritative
Definition
Management uses rewards. Information flowing upward is restricted to what management wants to hear and while policy decisions come from the top some prescribed decisions may be delegated to lower levels. Superiors expect subservience lower down.
Suitable for Property Investment?
No! You need to know what is going on at base level. The best people to know this, and hence set new policies, are the people dealing with

Management Style Benevolent authoritative

the tenants, agents, authorities, etc. You must listen to your employees who are dealing with these people so you can construct the right policies.

Management Style Consultative

Definition

Management offers rewards, occasional punishments. Big decisions come from the top while there is some wider decision-making involvement in details. Communication is downward while critical upward communication is cautious.

Suitable for Property Investment?

Maybe. This all depends on your employees. If they are self-starters, then this may not be applicable. If they need little supervision, believe in the common goal and are hard working, you can adopt the style below. Otherwise, consider this style to make sure that what you ask to be done gets done.

Management Style Participative group management

Definition

Management encourages group participation and involvement in setting high-performance goals with some economic rewards. Communication flows in all directions and is open and frank with decision making through group processes. All groups are linked to each other by persons who are members of more than one group, called 'linking pins'. Subordinates and superiors are close. The result is high productivity and better industrial relations.

Suitable for Property Investment?

Yes! To manage a property portfolio you need buy-in from ALL your staff where possible. If an employee has an idea, then find out the depth of it. If you have an idea, get buy-in from all your employees. Once you have people onside you will have the magical collective known as a TEAM! Once you're a team it will be very difficult to stop you.

Source: Likert, R. (1967), The Human Organization: Its Management and Value, McGrawHill. Material is reproduced with kind permission of The McGraw-Hill Companies.

The contractors

Whatever you do, do not consult your local *Yellow Pages* for a builder. There are numerous rogue contractors who spend a small fortune on advertising in the *Yellow Pages* posing as many different firms. You will ring around from the different ads, but ultimately you will speak to the same few contractors who employ this scam.

Builders

My advice is to use a builder from the National Federation of Builders (NFB) – see the Appendix for its contact details. The key features of the organisation and its members, as stated by the NFB on its website, are as follows:

- It's the industry's longest-established trade association with almost 3,000 member companies, ranging from small builders to large contractors.

- It has a network of regional offices across England and Wales and each one can provide a list of reputable, professional companies in your local area.

- Member companies of the NFB have satisfied the most stringent entrance criteria for any building trade association.

- Companies must provide at least eight references from accountants, previous clients, suppliers and professionals, such as architects and surveyors.

- All references are followed and, if satisfactory, applications are then put before a panel of existing members (who are local to the potential new member) for assessment.

- Every potential new member is also visited on site before they are accepted.

- If the panel is satisfied with the company's technical competence, health and safety standards and financial probity, the company is admitted into membership.

- All member companies must be VAT-registered (if applicable) and registered with the Construction Industry Training Board.

- The NFB also has a regional network of officers in the field meeting member companies day in, day out to ensure that the highest standards are being maintained.

- The NFB also operates a Code of Conduct and a full complaints procedure which involves a mediation and arbitration service. Complaints are thoroughly investigated by the NFB and if a member is found to be in breach of the Code of Conduct, he is expelled from the organisation.

- All NFB members can offer customers the 'Benchmark Plan' – an insurance-backed guarantee scheme which pays out the cost of correcting any building work defects for periods of up to 20 years.

Source: National Federation of Builders, www.builders.org.uk

It is also advisable to provide the builder you choose with a straightforward contract setting out in writing what is expected of you and him (e.g. payment terms and agreements) to help prevent any potential disputes. Lawpack publish a *Builder/Decorator Contract* which can be purchased on their website at www.lawpack.co.uk.

Plumbers

Again, avoid the *Yellow Pages*. Visit the Institute of Plumbing and Heating Engineering at www.iphe.org.uk; it has the same strict admission procedure for its members. The Institute's Top Ten tips for choosing a plumber are as follows:

1. Ask friends/relatives/neighbours whom they use.

2. Use a member of the Institute of Plumbing – members have to hold recognised qualifications in plumbing and/or have extensive experience.

3. Get at least three quotations when asking for quotations. Find out if there is a call-out fee, if more than one person will be doing the job and if so, if the price per hour includes all the workmen or if more is charged per plumber.

4. Ask for a written quotation. Unless there are any unforeseen costs, the final bill should not deviate too far from this initial written quotation.

5. Clearly explain all of the work you need doing and write it all down if possible.

6. Ask how long the job will take.

7. When you have found a plumber and the job is completed, ask for a full breakdown of the bill so you know where your money has gone.

8. Never pay upfront before a job is completed.

9. Good plumbers will be busy no matter when you call. Don't give up on quality to get a job finished quicker by someone else less qualified.

10. Don't be scared of asking questions – a registered plumber will be knowledgeable and able to answer anything you need to know.

Electricians

As with builders and plumbers you need to go to an electrician who is a member of a professional standards body. The National Inspection Council for Electrical Installation Contracting (NICEIC) was set up more than 45 years ago and is the electricity industry's independent, non-profit-making, voluntary regulatory body covering the whole of the UK. It's not a trade association and doesn't represent the interests of electrical contractors. In order to protect users of electricity, the NICEIC endeavours to register as many electrical contractors as possible who are able to comply with its rules. Every contractor who applies for registration is subjected to a detailed assessment by the NICEIC, including the technical standard of his electrical work, before being admitted to the Roll of Approved Contractors. It employs more than 50 area engineers who make annual visits to approved contractors to assess their technical capability and inspect samples of their electrical work.

You can find a suitable electrician in your area by visiting www.niceic.org.uk.

Your solicitor

Your solicitor should act for you and you only; he has to act in your best interests; any deviation from this and he is in breach of the Law Society rules. To ensure that you get the best from your solicitor or conveyancer, adopt the following principles:

Principle	Description
Fix the fee	Don't let him charge you on an hourly basis for his fees. If you choose a solicitor who specialises in conveyancing, he will know how long a purchase takes and should be able to quote you a ceiling-limit fee. Beware of hidden charges, such as for telephone calls and letters. Make sure that there are no hidden surprises.
Don't pay for insurance	Be careful of useless insurance policies as they add to the bill. Tell him that you don't want insurance covering you for unspotted defects. Then if the solicitor doesn't spot one, you can have a claim against him rather than the insurance company. A solicitor is more likely to pay out as no solicitor wants to incur the wrath of the Law Society.
Fee free for abortive purchases	Try to arrange a nil charge if the sale doesn't go through. This may be difficult if you are buying only one or two properties, but if you are buying a few and intend to buy in the future, then it's good to set up this arrangement. The worst thing is to have a solicitor's bill on top of survey costs for a property you have lost due to the vendor pulling out.
Pay for searches last	Where possible, apply for local searches last. This way if the purchase does fall through, you haven't paid out on searches in the meantime.

Principle	Description
Don't hassle him	Buying a property is a very slow process. There is no need to phone your solicitor every week. As long as you provide him with all the information he asks for, there is no need to call. If you have heard nothing for six weeks, then maybe it's worth a quick call for an update.
Make sure that he communicates with all the parties	Estate agents like to be kept up to date with a sale as their commission depends on it. If the agent doesn't hear anything from the solicitor, he will tell this to the vendor and sometimes the vendor places the property back on the market. Speak to the estate agent to ensure that he is getting feedback from the solicitor and is fully informed.

Find out whether your solicitor and the vendor's solicitor are in communication with each other through the estate agent. |
| Don't exchange contracts until the mortgage offer is received | Under no circumstances should you exchange without knowing that you have the funds to complete. This means a proper mortgage offer being received by your solicitor with all outstanding terms of the mortgage offer met. |

The mortgage broker

A good mortgage broker can be key to the whole buying process. It's not about getting the best deals. The difference between the best mortgage deal and the worst is nothing to write home about if you have bought at the right yield (see Chapter 1 – Yield for further information). It's all about getting your broker on your side.

Most brokers are small businesses and many dabble in the buy-to-let market, so they will understand your way of thinking. Here are some requests that you should make. They may seem a little bit pushy, but if he is a truly good broker, he should not be surprised by your requests – they assume that you are serious about property investment:

Request	Reason
Get him to fill out the forms	I hate filling out forms. I think we all do! I do about 100 remortgages and purchases and if I had to complete them all myself I probably wouldn't have the time to buy any properties! Brokers are only too willing to fill out these forms as they only have a chance to earn their commission if they submit a completed application form.
Let him tell you what to do	Take direction from him rather than you direct him. He knows what he's doing. My broker finds the lenders and I go with her recommendations. The only thing I decide on is what rate to go for. But I have to admit that if she told me what rate to go for, I would go for it no questions asked.
Try to avoid an upfront fee	This may not be possible in all circumstances as the best brokers do charge a fee. Try to get the broker to waive his fee after, say, ten deals a year.
Negotiate with estate agents	Try to get the broker to keep the agent updated on your case. The last thing you want is pushy agents ringing you up all the time asking questions that only your broker can answer.

If you're struggling to find a suitable broker, then try my one. I cannot promise she will grant you the same terms that I have (because I'm serious about property investment!) but it's worth a phone call. Contact Liz at Connect IFA on 01708 443 334 and mention my name and you'll get a 50 per cent discount on her fees.

The local authority

If you have decided to accept the low-paid, unemployed, sick or invalid as your tenant (which I suggest you do as the rent is paid directly to you and most tenants, even if they are on Housing Benefit, wish to make their property their home), most or all of your rent will be paid by the local authority. Getting the first rental payment from them can be a mission, but after that it's an easy ride. Let me tell you a little bit about how it works.

If you are a landlord wishing to rent out property, you may have tenants who are entitled to help toward paying the rent from their local council. Should a tenant make a claim for this help, called Housing Benefit, the local council will normally ask you for some simple information about the tenancy.

How Housing Benefit is calculated is described below, along with what information the tenant will be asked for and what information you will need to provide in order that an assessment of the level of Housing Benefit payable can be made.

What is Housing Benefit?

Housing Benefit is a government scheme administered by local councils that gives help towards housing costs for people on low incomes, including those who receive Income Support or Jobseeker's Allowance.

How is a claim made?

A claim is made by completing a Housing Benefit application form. The council can only discuss a benefit claim with a landlord if the tenant has given his permission in writing for this to be done.

What tenancy information is needed?

In addition to proof of income, every applicant for Housing Benefit must provide the following details:

- The date the tenancy started
- The date the tenant moved in
- The rent charged
- The number of rooms in the property
- The number of rooms occupied by the tenant
- The name and address of the landlord; and

- A tenancy agreement or a letter from the landlord showing the date the tenancy began, the amount of rent charged and any services included in the rent (e.g. heating, meals, etc.)

How much Housing Benefit will be paid?

Almost all claims for Housing Benefit are referred to the Rent Officer, who decides on a reasonable market rent for the property. Rent Officers are employed by the Government to help the council work out how much Housing Benefit a tenant can have. If a rent is considered to be unreasonably high, then the amount of Housing Benefit paid could be restricted. Housing Benefit may also be restricted because a tenant is living in a property which is larger than needed.

For example, a couple with one child need only two bedrooms, so their Housing Benefit may be restricted to the level for a two-bedroom house and not the three-bedroom house they actually occupy. The following criteria are used when deciding whether a property is or isn't too large.

One bedroom is allowed for each of the following:

- A married or unmarried couple
- A single person aged 16 or over
- Two children under the age of 16 of the same sex
- Two children under the age of 10
- A child under the age of 16

Housing Benefit cannot be paid for the part of the rent which covers services, such as water bills, fuel costs or meals. The costs of these items are deducted from the rent payable before Housing Benefit is calculated.

For example:

Actual rent charged	£80.00
Water bills	£5.00
Part-board (breakfast and evening meal)	£13.00
Eligible rent for Housing Benefit	£62.00

The net figure is called the 'eligible rent'. A person who receives Income Support could be entitled to full eligible rent. A person not on Income Support but on a low income will receive only part of the eligible rent.

Housing Benefit is always paid on a four-week cycle. If rent is charged on a per calendar month (pcm) basis, the appropriate weekly rent will be calculated and then paid on the usual four-week cycle.

For instance:

			£
Rent charged	=	500.00	per calender month
x 12	=	6,000.00	per year
÷ 365	=	16.438	per day
x 7	=	115.07	per week

So, if a tenant is entitled to full Housing Benefit, he would expect to receive £460.28 every four weeks, which is 4 x £115.07 weekly rent.

Pre-tenancy determination

If a tenant is looking for rented accommodation and needs to know how much of that rent will be used to work out his Housing Benefit before he decides to rent the property, he can apply for a free rent valuation called a 'pre-tenancy determination'. An application form for this must be completed by the prospective tenant and landlord and sent to the Rent Officer. When the form is returned, the Rent Officer may visit the property (if it hasn't been visited before) and then send a written decision to all the parties concerned.

How is Housing Benefit paid?

As previously mentioned, Housing Benefit is paid every four weeks, but, in most cases, it's four weeks in arrears. Housing Benefit is paid to the tenant unless a Rent Direct Form is completed, in which case the Benefit will be paid to the landlord.

If the Housing Benefit is paid to you as the landlord, you will also receive a schedule showing which tenants' Housing Benefit is included in the cheque and how much benefit is in respect of each tenant.

How long is Housing Benefit paid for?

All benefit claims are reviewed at least once a year, depending on the council's policy, but usually it's twice a year. The benefit will continue as long as there is entitlement providing the Claim Review Form is returned on time. Housing Benefit is only paid while a tenant lives in the property. Entitlement to benefit ends as soon as a tenant leaves the property. This condition also applies if a tenant dies, as entitlement ends on the date of death.

Entitlement may continue during a temporary absence from home. If a tenant moves out or dies and you have been paid Housing Benefit beyond your tenant's change of address or death, then you will have been overpaid and you will have to repay this money.

There may be times when the Housing Benefit Section finds out that a tenant has left before you do. Housing Benefit will still end on the date the tenant is known to have left – any further rent due is a matter for you to pursue with the tenant. Also, if the council finds out that he is working and is not entitled to Housing Benefit anymore, the council will come after you if they have paid the rent directly to you.

I have been the victim of this many a time. I have had to pay back to the council various amounts ranging from £70 to £2,400 because my tenants have been ineligible for Housing Benefit. The law has to change, as there are many landlords losing out due to these clawbacks. You have to decide whether you trust that the tenant will hand it over to you or whether you should get it paid directly to you but take the risk of a clawback. I always favour getting the rent paid direct and risking a clawback.

What does the council need from the landlord?

- Accurate information about the tenancy details including the start date, rent charged and any services provided.

- Prompt information regarding tenants moving out.

- Recognition by the landlord that the tenancy agreement is with the tenant. If there are difficulties with payment of rent, the landlord's first point of contact is the tenant.

- Prompt repayment of overpaid Housing Benefit.

Council Tax

Under normal circumstances the tenant is responsible for paying his Council Tax. If, however, the property is empty, then **you** are responsible for paying the Council Tax. The Council Tax departments of local authorities are hot! They know how to track you down to pay the tax, so there is no point avoiding their charge. If you do so, you could face being up in front of a magistrate and ultimately having your goods seized by registered bailiffs.

There are ways of reducing your Council Tax bill if the property becomes vacant:

- 100 per cent exemption for the first six months when the property becomes empty – unfurnished only; 50 per cent exemption for the following six months

- 50 per cent exemption for a vacant furnished property

- 100 per cent exemption for the duration the property is uninhabitable

Please ensure that you communicate to the council the status of the property to ensure that you can claim all the exemptions allowable to you.

The freeholder and managing agent

This section applies only to leasehold properties (e.g. flats and maisonettes) and is a book in itself. There have been many changes to the law giving more rights to leaseholders due to the unscrupulous behaviour of certain freeholders and managing agents. When I have seen criminal behaviour within property investment, the majority of times it has been within this sector.

Definitions

Term	Definition
Leaseholder	The leaseholder owns the right to occupy the premises for a certain period of time – typically 100 years. He is allowed 'quiet enjoyment' of his lease as you would expect with the ownership of any asset. He is expected to contribute to the maintenance of the building, the insurance and the cleaning of the common areas. He is also expected to pay a ground rent to the freeholder.
Freeholder	The freeholder owns the building and has granted leases to the various leaseholders. The building belongs to him, but he has no right of access to any areas covered in your lease. He only has access to the common areas. The freeholder is your landlord and expects the ground rent from you and any costs associated with the building. He can take your lease away from you (through a lengthy court procedure) if you consistently breach the terms of the lease.
Managing agent	If the freeholder wishes to outsource the management of the building, he can instruct a managing agent to handle the day-to-day organisation of cleaning, maintenance, building works and administration.

The freeholder or managing agent will send you a bill for the ground rent and service charge either monthly, quarterly, half-yearly or annually. Some will charge you what they think they can get away with. I have a flat where the service charge is more than the mortgage!

If you get extortionate service charge bills, you can do the following:

Action	Description
Not pay	The service charge has to be reasonable. If the managing agent has charged you £50 for changing a light bulb in the common area, then this is

Action	Description
	excessive. Reasonableness is determined by the Fair Value Tribunal (FVT). If you think that it's unreasonable, you can wait for the managing agent to take the matter to the FVT.
	You must write to the managing agent to dispute his charge. Don't simply refuse to pay. I have one managing agent who charges me 29.5 per cent APR on late payment, £23.50 per letter or email sent, which he sends every week, and he charges me £48 per hour for his time in dealing with my case. I haven't paid him for any of these charges. I have simply paid the service charge without all of his fees added on. He hasn't taken me to court as I know that the tribunal or court would laugh at his extortionate charges.
Offer a settlement	Just pay what you think is reasonable. It will be down to the managing agent to take you to the FVT or court for the difference. If the court deems that what he is charging is correct, then you will have to pay up as you will not want to lose your lease. Usually he won't take you to court and you can carry on paying what you think is fair.
Ask for the financial statements	The managing agent has to provide you with the latest financial statements within 28 days of your request, otherwise it is a criminal offence. If you dispute the service charge bill, look at the expenses that he is incurring. Then you can pinpoint where the overcharge is – it's usually the management fees!
	You are well within your right to visit the premises to inspect each and every invoice that make up those accounts and to challenge them.
Seek outside help	The obvious place to go is to your solicitor, but there are other organisations that can help, such as www.lease-advice.org.uk, www.leaseholdadvice. co.uk or www.arma.org.uk.

Your accountant

If you have instructed an accountant to handle your affairs because the thought of filling in your own Tax Return seems too daunting, you will then have to manage him. Ensure that you do the following:

Action	Description
Go to an accountant who has been recommended to you	This is the best way to get anyone to do work for you. If you can afford one, go for a chartered or certified accountant. If you can't find one from a recommendation, then visit www.icaew.co.uk or www.acca.co.uk to find the nearest accountant in your area.
Get all the information to the accountant on time	In order that your accountant can give your case the time it deserves, ensure that you provide him with all of the information on time. I know this sounds obvious, but you would be surprised how many people leave their tax affairs until the last minute – including me! If you can get your form in by 30 September, the Inland Revenue will calculate your tax for you.
Find out if he is knowledgeable in land and property tax	In order to pay the least tax, he should know how to obtain all the reliefs due to you in order to shelter your profits. Ask him if he has any clients who are involved in property investment. See if he is aware of allowances such as the 'wear and tear' allowance for furnished properties.
Agree the fee in advance	Don't let him charge you by the hour. Once you have shown him your type of records, the size of operations and number of transactions, it should be easy for him to calculate the fee. Be clear about what you want from your accountant; is it just your Tax Return completion or the whole package including book-keeping, payroll, etc.?

The law

There are two other categories of law you have to adhere to, apart from the standard contractual law that exists between a landlord and tenant under the Housing Act 1988:

- Regulatory
- All-encompassing

Regulatory

There are three main regulations governing the renting of properties:

1. Gas safety
2. Electrical safety
3. Fire resistance

Gas safety

As the landlord you must ensure that all gas appliances, fittings and flues provided for use are safe. As a landlord, you must ensure that:

- gas fittings, appliances (including portable ones like LPG cabinet heaters and those serving relevant premises but installed elsewhere) pipe-work and flues are maintained in a safe condition;
- all installation, maintenance and safety checks are carried out by a CORGI-registered gas installer;
- an annual safety check is carried out on each gas appliance/flue by a CORGI-registered gas installer. Checks need to have taken place within one year of the start of the tenancy/lease date, unless the appliances have been installed for less than 12 months, in which case they should be checked within 12 months of their installation date;
- a record of each safety check is kept for two years;
- a copy of the current safety check record, which can be either a

CORGI Landlord's Gas Safety Record or something similar, is issued to each existing tenant within 28 days of the check being completed, or to any new tenant before he moves in (in certain cases, such as holiday property, the record can be displayed).

CORGI recommends that all gas appliances are serviced annually. Please note that an appliance service inspection will not necessarily provide sufficient information to meet the needs of the landlord's annual safety check, nor will an annual safety check necessarily be sufficient to provide effective maintenance. Always ask the advice of a CORGI-registered installer. To find a CORGI-registered installer in your area visit www.corgi-group.com or call 0870 401 2300.

Source: CORGI (Council for Registered Gas Installers)

Electrical safety

At present there is no requirement for the property to be checked for electrical safety. However, the law can always change. Also with the number of Claims Direct 'no win, no fee' type of companies growing all the time, the likelihood of your tenant suing you for electric shock injuries will also increase. A good defence is to have the property inspected by an official electrical contractor every year. It is also advisable for all of the electrical appliances supplied with the property to be inspected by an NICEIC contractor annually.

You can find out where your nearest NICEIC contractor is by visiting www.niceic.org.uk.

Fire resistance

All upholstered furniture has to comply with the Furniture and Furnishings (fire) (safety) Regulations 1988. To tell if it is compliant, check the label in the cushioning, but you shouldn't have a problem with any furniture purchased after 1990 as they will automatically comply with the regulations.

The law applies to:

- armchairs, three-piece suites, sofas, sofa beds, futons and other convertible furniture;
- beds, bed bases and headboards, mattresses, divans and pillows;
- nursery furniture;
- garden furniture which could be used indoors;
- loose, stretch and fitted covers for furniture, scatter cushions, seat pads and pillows.

Excluded items

The regulations do **not** currently apply to:

- antique furniture or furniture manufactured before 1950;
- bedclothes and duvets;
- loose mattress covers;
- pillowcases;
- sleeping bags;
- curtains;
- carpets.

Compliance

Furniture which complies carries a manufacturer's label which must be permanent and non-detachable.

- All upholstered items must have fire-resistant filling material.
- All upholstered items must pass the 'match resistance test' as prescribed.
- All upholstered items must also pass the 'cigarette test' as prescribed.
- Bed bases and mattresses are not required to bear a permanent label, but compliance will be indicated if the item has a label stating that it meets BS7177.

All-encompassing

Outside of the regulations governing landlords mentioned above, we all have to abide by the laws of the land whether one is a landlord or not. Specifically a landlord will have to be aware of the following:

1. The law of tort – negligence and personal injury

2. Criminal law

The law of tort

This part of the law ensures that if anyone suffers an injury, the person responsible (if any) is brought to justice and ordered to pay damages to the injured party. You, as a landlord, are liable to pay damages to the injured party if:

1. your tenant or anyone entering your investment property suffered an injury; and

2. you owed a duty of care to the person entering your investment property who suffered the personal injury; and

3. you breached that duty of care.

As an example, if you fail to fix the light socket and a guest of your tenant suffers an electric shock burn, you will have to compensate the guest because he was injured. It is realistically expected that your tenant will invite a guest into the property and it is your responsibility as landlord to fix the socket when your tenant asks you to.

Criminal law

This covers:

- Violence

- Harassment

- Evictions without a court order

Violence

Violence can never be the answer in any situation. You may get frustrated with a tenant who simply refuses to pay, but resorting to violence will turn a financial problem into an even greater problem, even possibly a prison sentence. Remember, it's only money! Always allow yourself a calming-down period. If it has gone beyond your ability to remain calm, then get someone else to do the negotiating.

Harassment

You cannot:

- ring/visit your tenant repeatedly or at unsociable hours demanding payment;
- cut off essential services such as water, gas and electricity;
- make threats of violence to any member of the household.

The court takes this type of behaviour (harassment) very seriously and so they should! If a tenant gets into financial difficulty, this does not give you the right to treat him in an unsavoury manner.

Evictions without a court order

The only way you can evict a tenant is with a court order. Without a court order the eviction becomes a criminal offence. You have to serve the right notices at the right times and follow court rules. Failure to do this will mean a court order will not be granted. The law is complicated so to ensure that all rules are followed, instruct a solicitor who specialises in this area.

CHAPTER 3

Gearing

We are in a low-interest environment. To me, low interest means below eight per cent base rate and 9.5 per cent actual borrowing rate. Now, you may think this is high, but this was the rate when deals were made as far back as 1997 when I first started. Then you could buy a studio flat within the M25 for less than £30,000 and rent it out at £350 per calendar month (pcm). Looking at this equation the profit was:

Rent	£350
£30,000 purchase: mortgage @ 85% Loan To Value @ 9.5% interest only	£202
Service charge	£40
Profit	**£108**

Now, this does not seem much, but looking at the gross yield, in Year 2 after acquisition costs have been paid, it's:

£350 x 12	=	£4,200	=	14% yield
Purchase	=	£30,000		

which is fantastic and let's look at the return on cash in Year 2:

£108 x 12	=	£1,296	=	29% ROCE
£30,000 x 15%	=	£4,500		

So borrowing at 9.5 per cent interest rates back in 1997 was a good thing EVEN though the rates were so high! At a 9.5 per cent borrowing rate, you can still get a 29 per cent return on your money. If you had left the money in the bank, you would have received only eight per cent. So by borrowing and investing in property you more than treble your return. The key to all of this is that the gross yield is in excess of 12 per cent.

The correlation between yield, ROCE and the interest rate

The main reason why I set my target as 12 per cent yield is because it's easy to calculate whether a property is a 12 per cent yielder. Let me show you:

If you see a property advertised for £50,000 and it's a 12 per cent yielder, it should rent out for £500pcm (i.e. you knock off the two zeros of the purchase price and it gives you the expected rent). So if you find out that it rents out at £600pcm, you buy it without looking at it! If you find out it rents out at £300pcm, you forget about it!

Now for the science. Look at the following table. It details the ROCE based on the yield and interest rate being charged. I've assumed full occupancy, no repairs and £10pcm building insurance.

ROCE based on yield and the interest rate (85 per cent gearing)

		Yield								
		4%	5%	6%	7%	8%	9%	10%	11%	12%
Interest	5%	−2.5	4.2	10.9	17.5	24.2	30.9	37.5	44.2	50.9
Rate	6%	−8.1	−1.5	5.2	11.9	18.5	25.2	31.9	38.5	45.2
	7%	−13.8	−7.1	−0.5	6.2	12.9	19.5	26.2	32.9	39.5
	8%	−19.5	−12.8	−6.1	0.5	7.2	13.9	20.5	27.2	33.9
	9%	−25.1	−18.5	−11.8	−5.1	1.5	8.2	14.9	21.5	28.2
	10%	−30.8	−24.1	−17.5	−10.8	−4.1	2.5	9.2	15.9	22.5

If you look at the five per cent interest rate row (which is approximately the current buy-to-let borrowing rate), you can see that the ROCE increases with the yield. If you look at it even closer, you will see that with every one per cent increase in yield the ROCE increases by 6.6–6.7 per cent (actually 6.667 per cent without rounding).

This is why yield is important. It's easy to think 'Oh, there's not much difference between an eight per cent and a nine per cent yielding property', but there is – 6.667 per cent ROCE!

So why do I say 12 per cent yield? Well, look at the 12 per cent yielding column. At current interest rates of five per cent, your ROCE is a very nice 50.9 per cent. Even at interest rates of ten per cent, your ROCE is still a very nice 22.5 per cent, even though you are in a high-interest-rate environment. However, if you buy at eight per cent yield, which is still quite a respectable yield, your ROCE is making a loss at −4.1 per cent, plus you are assuming the property to be fully occupied and not in need of repair!

In a rising-interest-rate environment, investors who have purchased from four to six per cent yields will be forced to sell as they hold a liability (i.e. it will cost them money to own the property) rather than an asset (i.e. it's earning them money), which is what they initially thought they were buying!

Now that we've established that we should be aiming for a 12 per cent yield, let's now focus on the level of borrowing. Take a look at the same table as above, but this time with only a 50 per cent level of borrowing:

ROCE based on yield and the interest rate (50 per cent gearing)

		Yield								
		4%	5%	6%	7%	8%	9%	10%	11%	12%
Interest	5%	2.8	4.8	6.8	8.8	10.8	12.8	14.8	16.8	18.8
Rate	6%	1.8	3.8	5.8	7.8	9.8	11.8	13.8	15.8	17.8
	7%	−4.1	−2.1	−0.1	1.9	3.9	5.9	7.9	9.9	16.8
	8%	−5.8	−3.8	−1.8	0.2	2.2	4.2	6.2	8.2	15.8
	9%	−7.5	−5.5	−3.5	−1.5	0.5	2.5	4.5	6.5	14.8
	10%	−9.2	−7.2	−5.2	−3.2	−1.2	0.8	2.8	4.8	13.8

Looking at the five per cent interest rate row, we can see that the ROCE for a 12 per cent yielding property is 18.8 per cent. Comparing this to the ROCE of 50.9 per cent for 85 per cent gearing above, you can see that if you raise your borrowing by 35 per cent (i.e. from 50 per cent to 85 per cent gearing), you almost triple your ROCE!

Now take a look at the ROCEs for a borrowing level of nil, 50 per cent, 85 per cent and 100 per cent for a 12 per cent yielding property:

Interest Rate	Nil LTV	50% LTV	85% LTV	100% LTV
5%	12%	18.8%	50.9%	Infinity
6%	12%	17.8%	45.2%	Infinity
7%	12%	16.8%	39.5%	Infinity
8%	12%	15.8%	33.9%	Infinity
9%	12%	14.8%	28.2%	Infinity
10%	12%	13.8%	22.5%	Infinity

Here we can clearly see that the ROCE increases rapidly the more we borrow and if we don't borrow, all we can expect to make on the ROCE is the yield itself. The table also shows that the ROCE grows from 50.9 per cent at 85 per cent gearing to infinity at 100 per cent gearing. It seems strange that this extra 15 per cent level of borrowing would make such a difference, but it does!

OK, I want you to follow this one simple rule and then you are ensured a steady path to property millionairedom:

IF THE YIELD IS IN EXCESS OF 12 PER CENT, THEN BORROW THE MOST YOU CAN!

Take a look at this graph:

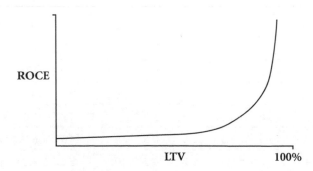

You can see that the closer you get to 100 per cent LTV financing, your ROCE tends to infinity. So if you want to maximise your ROCE, you should aim as close as you can to 100 per cent financing. I started with £500 seven years ago and I bought a house worth £49,000 with this amount, which equates to 99 per cent financing. If I sold up now I would net £3m after clearing all that I borrowed. My ROCE over the seven years is:

$$\frac{£3 \text{ million}}{£500} \times 100 = 600,000\%$$

Now I know 600,000 per cent isn't infinity, but it's not bad!

Achieving 100 per cent LTV financing

How can you do this? Well, let's look at how you are expected to fund a buy-to-let property:

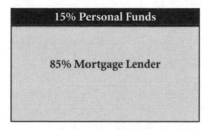

The majority of the purchase price comes from a mortgage lender and the rest from you. There is a very good reason why the banks expect you to contribute. Take a look at this next graph:

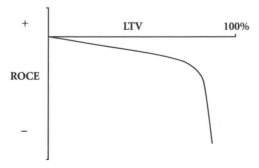

This shows the ROCE if the tenant didn't pay you any rent at all. You can see that as the borrowing increases, the ROCE tends to minus infinity! This is how people go out of business very quickly. If they have overborrowed and the cash doesn't come in on time or at all, then it's game over. The bank's job is to make sure that you don't overborrow. They do this is by lending you only 85 per cent of the purchase price and making you come up with the rest to ensure that they don't encounter a minus infinity situation.

However, making you come up with the other 15 per cent restricts the number of purchases you can make, so if you wish to buy a £100,000 property, you must come up with £15,000 out of your personal funds. This is not an easy task. On an average salary of £20,000, realistically it would take you three years to save this kind of deposit and if you could only buy a property every three years, there's no point giving up your day job as it wouldn't be until retirement age before you could say goodbye to the rat race and retire on the income produced from your property portfolio.

If you did find a lender that would lend you 100 per cent, you could theoretically buy all the properties in the world subject to your credit limit and there would be nothing to stop you earning what you desired. The only thing that would limit you is the time to actually acquire all these properties! What a luxury to be constrained only by time and not money. The truth is that this luxury is achievable but you have to be brave, believe in your abilities and be willing to persist.

Achieving the 15 per cent deposit

If you want to grow quickly, then you need to access the other 15 per cent as soon as possible! As described in my other book, *The Buy-to-Let Bible* (Lawpack), in more detail, the deposit can be raised quickly in four ways:

Vendor incentives

Vendor gift

This is where you basically get the mortgage lender to pay most of your deposit! For example, you would like to purchase an investment property advertised for £54,000, but you can only get your hands on £3,000 for a deposit. As a result, you ask the vendor if he will inflate the purchase price to £60,000 and include a £6,000 vendor deposit, thus creating the £9,000 deposit you require.

Without the vendor gift you have a shortfall of £5,100, but with it you don't. The vendor is also happy as he still gets the asking price:

£60,000 minus £6,000 = £54,000

Your borrowings are now almost 100 per cent loan to value (LTV), which you are receiving totally from the mortgage lender.

This trick is completely legal, but relies on the property being valued up to £60,000. This is likely because of three reasons:

1. Valuers don't like to down-value a property.

2. You may be getting a bargain property.

3. Valuers are under pressure to value properties at the purchase price.

Note: Remember that the vendor must declare the inflated sales price to the Inland Revenue and may have to pay more Capital Gains Tax. However, the Inland Revenue gives you an individual exemption allowance of £8,200 so if the inflated price doesn't take the gain above this allowance, he will not have to pay any extra tax.

Cashback

Like a vendor gift, cashback works in the same way. In the above example the deal would be structured as:

£60,000 purchase price + £9,000 cashback

In this instance, when you buy the property you put down £9,000 as your deposit, which you may have borrowed on your credit card, and you get £9,000 back when you complete the purchase enabling you to pay back your credit card company.

100 per cent plus mortgages

If you find saving too painful, then there are mortgage companies that will lend you the whole amount. There are even lenders out there who will loan you more than the value of the purchase price because they believe that the excess amount over the purchase price can be used to improve the property and, as a result, will push up the value of the house. However, you do have to aim to live in it. Therefore, the theory is to buy the property as a residential property and then inform the lender after the deal is completed that you want to let it out.

This is best explained with the following example:

Joanne, who has no deposit, decides to buy a property for £100,000, but the kitchen and bathroom is in poor repair. She gets an estimate for the work and she finds a builder that will do the whole job for £5,000. Joanne decides to go for the property and applies for a 105 per cent mortgage. This means that she will get:

* £100,000 to purchase the property

* £5,000 to repair the property

After the repair, the property will be worth £110,000–£120,000 as the property is more saleable now due to it being more presentable to the market. Depending on the lender, she can now inform him that she wishes to let it out. If he agrees, he will charge her anywhere between £nil to a two per cent loading on the interest rate. If this fee is too much, she can then remortgage the property on a buy-to-let mortgage. If it gets valued at £120,000, he will lend her £102,000. This will clear most of the original £105,000 balance leaving a shortfall of £3,000, which she will have to contribute to. So, in effect, she gets a £120,000 property for £3,000 – that's 97.5 per cent financing!

Loans

You can get a loan instantly by simply borrowing it! I suggest that you only take on this credit (if you are borrowing from a credit card or bank) after your mortgage application has been submitted and you have been credit-checked, otherwise this borrowing will show up. This in itself may not be a problem, but if you can, try to get it after submission.

You can get a deposit from the following sources:

Source	Description
Remortgaging current assets	• **Your personal home** – This is the cheapest form of borrowing you can get. You may be sitting on a nice little nest egg, but doing nothing with it. If you have got equity in your home, then get to it and put it to work! There are literally thousands of deals, far more than buy-to-let deals, for personal residential mortgages. I have even seen introductory rates of 0.99 per cent. These introductory rates are perfect for when you start the property investment game as it gives you the breathing space in the initial months to carry out any work required on the property. • **Your investment properties** – If you have any investment properties, remortgage them up to the hilt. If you believe in your investment decisions, get the cash and buy more. Don't worry about the mortgage payment increasing on the original property as the profit made on the future purchases will fully compensate this increase and more!
Credit card companies	**Your credit card company** – They have had a lot of bad press in the past but this is the fault of the cardholder, not the company. The key to playing the credit card game is having a plan to pay them back. Many businesses have been funded by credit cards during the bad times and have saved companies going bankrupt, but you never hear about it in the press as it doesn't make good news. I have several credit cards with a total credit limit of £13,000 which I only ever use in times of necessity. A couple of years ago, I used

Source	Description
	my credit cards to buy a really cheap investment property as they advance you the cash immediately. Careful use of my credit cards has made me £15,000 profit!

Credit card companies are begging us to borrow, so much so that they offer 0 per cent for balance transfers. The trick to obtaining your deposit is to:

- apply and obtain for a standard credit card;
- withdraw cash on this card to the full amount;
- apply and obtain a 0 per cent APR credit card;
- transfer the balance on the standard card to the 0 per cent APR card;
- pay off the balance before the introductory period is over;
- if the introductory period expires, apply, obtain and transfer the balance to another 0 per cent APR card.

You can only start this process after you have submitted your application form and have been credit-checked by the mortgage lender.

Yet please, please, please note: CREDIT CARDS ARE EXPENSIVE when you either default or go over the introductory period. Have a plan on how you are going to pay back this balance and for how long.

If you don't, you may end up in unmanageable debt and then the whole property investment game, with all its associated debts, will become a nightmare.

Note: Barclaycard offer a lifetime period of 0 per cent until the debt is repaid, but this requires you to have a minimum spend per month.

One way to plan the repayment of the credit card balance is to take up a cashback mortgage, which gives you cash when you buy the property on completion.

Source	Description
Overdraft facilities	**Your overdraft provider** – This involves the same principle as the credit card trick. You simply obtain the deposit from your overdraft provider and pay it back within a set time period.
	You may be able to get an overdraft facility from your bank. Simply ask! They will need to see your salary being deposited every week or month for a period of at least six months. This should not pose a problem if they have been your bank for more than six months.
	Unlike credit cards, they don't offer introductory rates so they do work out to be expensive. They usually start from five per cent above the Bank of England Base Rate, so at today's rates they start from 8.5 per cent and can rise to as high as 15 per cent. The beauty of an overdraft, however, is that it can be redeemed whenever you want to. A good way to redeem it is with a cash-gift mortgage like a cashback mortgage.
Personal loans	**Your loan provider** – You can raise the deposit by simply taking out a loan. The loan will be paid back over a number of years in equal instalments. However, you must consider whether you can pay back the loan and the mortgage in total, otherwise there is no point!
	For example, if you need £5,000 to put down for a £95,000 mortgage, your total cost of borrowing will be:

£5,000 loan	£111.45
£95,000 mortgage	£412.98
Total	**£524.43**

Do make sure that you can afford both the repayments. Unlike the credit cards and overdrafts, a loan is less easier to redeem as there are penalties. Sometimes the penalties are not too extortionate so it may be worth redeeming the

Source	Description
	loan with a penalty in order to save on the interest you will pay over the duration of the loan.
	Some lenders require a second charge on your personal property. This is not a problem, but be really careful of their redemption penalties. If they are in excess of five per cent of the loan, then steer clear as these penalties can ultimately trap you in your home.
	Be sure to apply for the loan after submitting your mortgage application form.
Loan from friend or family	**Your family** – I have been on both sides of this equation! I have borrowed and been borrowed from. In the first instance, I borrowed £500 from my Mum to kick-start my first property purchase. In the second instance, I loaned £1,800 to one of my good friends in order to clear his credit card debt. He immediately paid me back using his credit card chequebook when the mortgage completed!
	You will be surprised how helpful the people are around you. I suggest approaching your family members first and then moving outside of the family once all avenues have been exhausted. Do offer them an attractive rate of interest as no-one does anything for nothing!

Get a partner

Another way to raise the cash is to take on a financial partner. This can be a disadvantage as although the financial risk is borne by the partner, you end up doing all the work. The partner will be entitled to a share of your profits and you won't be free to do what you want with the property.

Equating the cost to you will depend on how successful the property is as the cost will be the share of the profits made. Even though this is the most expensive way to finance a property business, it can also be the cheapest way as your partner has taken the full financial risk if the whole project fails. If this is the only method you can use to get into property, I still advise taking on a partner as you will still be participating in a share of the property market.

However, do consider the drawbacks that joint ownership brings:

1. The loss of full freedom of sole ownership. When you have to sell, you will need to get your partner to agree on whether you want to sell and the price.

2. The gain on the property will have to be shared with your partner.

3. You will be liable for the mortgage payments if your partner defaults.

I am involved in a TV programme which is exactly about this concept. First-time buyers will be put together so that they can purchase their first home together and sell within two years, make a gain, split the gain and then use this gain to buy their own property individually. You can use a partner in this way and both benefit. However, it's worth planning the exit route and you should only enter into this type of agreement with people you trust.

My real-life experiences

I have used all of these four methods in order to raise a deposit. Let me give you a history of what I've done:

Trick	Description
Vendor gift	I bought a house for £30,000 plus a £1,500 vendor deposit. This had two effects: I had to put down less as I was getting a £1,500 vendor deposit and it took the purchase price to the £30,000 bracket, where you can get higher LTVs.
Cashback	I bought a house for £40,000 plus £2,500 cashback. Again, I had to put down less as I was getting a cash gift of £2,500. I had to put the £2,500 down initially, but I got it straight back after completion.

Trick	Description
Cashback mortgage	My first house was bought on a cashback mortgage. I had to put five per cent down as a deposit to get five per cent cashback. I simply borrowed the five per cent using my overdraft facility, approximately £2,500, and got the £2,500 back when I completed.
92 per cent residential mortgage	The second property I bought was on a residential mortgage. I had to put ten per cent down as a deposit to get two per cent cashback. When it completed, I got a two per cent cashback, around £1,000, and then told the lender that I wished to rent it out. He charged me a £75 annual letting fee and granted me permission to let it out.
Remortgage personal home	I'm always doing this! I recently remortgaged my house to 90 per cent LTV, the maximum my lender would go to, to access another £35,000 and with the money I used it as five deposits of £7,000 each in order to buy another five houses!
Remortgage investment properties	I'm always doing this too! I aim to keep my portfolio at 85 per cent LTV of its current market value. Recently, I instructed my broker to carry out 31 remortgages in one hit, which certainly kept her busy!
Credit cards	As mentioned earlier in the book, I accessed £13,000 (the maximum credit limit I have over three credit cards) to fund deposits for new purchases. When the remortgages came through on some other properties, I paid back the credit card balances. The cost of borrowing was no more than £500 and the amount I made on the deal was £15,000. Who said credit cards are bad?
Overdrafts	As mentioned earlier, I used my overdraft for short-term funding purposes. Remember that overdraft facilities have a maximum term,

Trick	Description
	usually one year, and have to be renewed. Don't get caught out and be forced to pay back the overdraft due to the fact that you never checked when the facility expired.
Unsecured loans	I have over £100,000 in personal loans. I got these at the time I was starting. The properties that I have bought with this money have netted me around £500,000 in equity. Now that's not bad by anyone's standards!
Borrow off girlfriend	I sail very close to the wind sometimes and I got into a situation. I was once forced into going to a bridging finance company who were going to charge me 22 per cent APR and £1,000 in arrangement fees to borrow £10,000. To avoid this, I decided to ask my girlfriend instead and I offered her 16 per cent APR. She generously agreed and I paid her back in three months plus interest AS WELL AS a set of diamond earrings!
Get a partner	I'm currently doing a deal with someone who has money, but not the expertise. He will be fronting all the money and I will be investing it. We'll be going 50:50 on ownership and the profits generated. I'm doing this because it's a sizeable amount of money, which will give me a greater market share than I already have – this is why it works for me.

The cost of holding money

I hate having money! Now, when I say this, I mean that I hate having money that's uninvested. Not only is anything in excess of float not making you any money, but it's costing you as well. For example, if I go out and raise £10,000 on an unsecured loan repayable over five years, I then have to start making payments of around £200pcm one month after the bank has advanced me the money. If I don't find an investment, I will have to pay back 60 months x £200 = £12,000, which isn't good business.

If I find an investment property the day I get the money (requiring a £10,000 deposit), complete on the purchase three months later and find a tenant one month after that, which provides me a positive cashflow of £100pcm, then the figures look like this:

Positive cashflow from investment: 56 months x £100	£5,600
Cost of holding: four months x £200	(£800)
Profit arising from £10,000 loan	**£4,800**

There are two important things to notice about this example:

1. £4,800 profit is generated from taking out the £10,000 over five years. Even more profit will be generated after the five years due to the loan being redeemed, thus increasing the cashflow, assuming that all the other factors remain the same.

2. The profit is reduced by £800 due to it taking four months to complete on the property and to find a tenant.

As a result of these findings, two principles will hold:

1. It's good to borrow; and

2. the quicker you make the investment the more money you make.

Now I'm not saying go out and buy the next property that comes onto the market. What makes sense is to try to find suitable property investments before you get the loan and as far as possible try to line up a tenant in advance.

The opportunity cost of money

'Opportunity cost is a term used in economics to mean the cost of something in terms of an opportunity foregone (and the benefits that could be received from that opportunity), or the most valuable forgone alternative.

For example, if a city decides to build a hospital on vacant land that it owns, the opportunity cost is some other thing that might have been done with the land and construction funds instead. In building the hospital, the city has forgone the opportunity to build a sporting center on that land, or a parking lot, or the ability to sell the land to reduce the city's debt, and so on. In more personal terms, the opportunity cost of spending a Friday night drinking with your friends could be the amount of money you could have earned if you had devoted that time to working overtime. This does not always mean something of monetary value, just anything that is of any value to the subject in question.'

Source: www.wikipedia.org

Let me explain. I specialise in low-value properties and I usually buy a property for approximately £30,000. This requires me to put forward an initial investment of £5,000, which includes the deposit, legal fees, etc. Every time I get hold of £5,000, I'm itching to buy a property.

Now consider this. I'm walking past a car showroom and I see my favourite car, a Mercedes 300SL, for the bargain price of £20,000. I've got the money so should I buy it? If I buy it for cash, it won't cost me £20,000. It will actually cost me what I will lose in the future as a result of the purchase. This will be the following:

Purchase price of car	£20,000
Initial investment for a house	£5,000
Number of houses that can be bought: £20,000 ÷ £5,000	4
Expected profit generated from each property	£150pcm
Total profit expected from four properties	**£600pcm**

So if I buy the car for cash, I will lose £600pcm. This comes to £7,200 per year and excludes capital growth. If the houses have risen by ten per cent in the year, the capital growth will be 4 x £30,000 x 10 per cent = £12,000. This results in the total loss, including capital growth, being £12,000 + £7,200 = £19,200, which is almost the cost of the car! And what would the car be worth in a year? Well, it won't be worth more than £20,000, that's for sure! Let's say £15,000.

So let's look at the true loss of buying a car relative to buying four investment properties after one year:

Net worth after buying car – market value of car	£15,000
Net worth after buying four properties: Four deposits x £4,500	£18,000
Rental profit	£7,200
Capital growth	£12,000
Total	**£37,200**

After one year the difference in net worth of buying a car and investing in four properties is:

£37,200 minus £15,000 = **£22,200**

That's an annual salary for someone! If the £20,000 I had in the bank was due to a remortgage, then the figures are even worse. £20,000 borrowed at five per cent makes you a further £1,000 worse off and if you don't redeem the debt after one year, it will cost you £1,000 year after year after year. If you let it run until the end of your mortgage term, you may end up paying more interest than the price of the car!

I'll be honest with you, however. I do own a Mercedes 300SL worth £20,000, but you'll be damn sure I didn't pay for it in cash! I bought the car on HP at 17.3 per cent APR. It costs me £462 per month, which is paid for out of my £600pcm profits generated from my property purchases.

The principle is: preserve your cash! If you can get sensible credit (less than 20 per cent APR), take it. As long as you are willing to invest the money you have, you can always service the credit you get with the profits you generate.

CHAPTER 4

Awareness

The actual price of a property is made up of two elements – the real price of the property and the bubble element:

'Pactual' = 'Preal' + 'Pbubble'

Pactual: The current market value of the property

Preal: The real price of a property based on fundamental principles

Pbubble: The surplus or deficit of the actual price over the real price

In a perfect market, the actual price of a property should equal the real price of a property. Unfortunately, this never happens! This is because we live in an imperfect market which is driven by people's own opinions and views (including mine!) that are impossible to predict.

The key to property investment is **never** to buy a property at a price where there is a bubble element to it, i.e. make sure that the Pbubble = 0 or less. In order to determine each element, firstly we must determine the current market value of the property; secondly, work out the real value of the property; and thirdly, calculate the bubble element, which is the difference between the actual and the real value of the property.

Pactual: The current market value of the property

On average, properties sell at 95 per cent of their asking price so we will determine the current market value to be this percentage of the advertised price of a property. This is the only way you are going to get an up-to-date value of a property as best you can. The Land Registry figures are too out of date to really use as a current market value as there is around a nine-month lag from the agreed offer price to the published price.

Preal: The real price of a property based on fundamental principles

The real price of a property is based on two fundamental principles. It is either the greater of:

1. the price willing to be paid by an investor; or

2. the price willing to be paid by a first-time buyer.

Whichever is the greater out of these two figures will be the real price of the property. Therefore, we need to calculate both of these prices.

The price willing to be paid by an investor

The price willing to be paid by an investor will be dependent on what he can get elsewhere in the market. If he didn't want to take a risk, he would just stick the money in the bank and earn interest, but as he's investing in property he will expect a premium for his risk-taking. As property is a long-term investment, he will compare this timescale with one that is risk free. The best rates he would get would be from a:

20-year fixed-interest government gilt

A government gilt is a loan to the Government. As it is assumed that the Government will never go bankrupt, it is deemed to be risk free. Property is then considered to be the next lowest risk investment out there. On average, property investors accept a lot less than me and only require a two per cent loading on top of a 20-year fixed government gilt in order for them to invest. Here loading means the extra return required in order to take the risk. Two per cent is an average – some investors require more, some may need less.

This loading will determine the yield required and hence set the real value of the property. Let's look at an example:

Variables:

20-year fixed interest government gilt	5.62%
Property investor loading	2%
Annual rental value of the property	**£5,000**

The real value would be:

$$\frac{£5,000}{(5.62\% + 2\%)} = £65,616$$

This is the maximum value an investor would be willing to pay for a property with a rental value of £5,000. If the property price was higher, the investor would place it in a risk-free investment (e.g. a government gilt).

The property price may be higher due to a first-time buyer being able to **afford** the property.

The price willing to be paid by a first-time buyer

The price willing to be paid by a first-time buyer will be:

$$\frac{\text{His salary} \times 4}{(0.95)}$$

This assumes that a lender will lend him four times his salary if he puts down a five per cent deposit on the property. So, in the same example above, if a first-time buyer wants the same property and his salary is £21,000, he can afford a purchase price of:

$$\frac{(£21,000 \times 4)}{(0.95)} = £88,421$$

So in this example the first-time buyer 'wins' and, as a result, the real value of the property is £88,421.

Pbubble: The surplus or deficit of the actual price over the real price

The bubble element is simply the difference between the actual and real prices:

$$Pactual\ minus\ Preal = Pbubble$$

Using the above example, assuming that the actual price is £95,000 and the real price is £88,421, the bubble element will be:

$$£95,000\ minus\ £88,421 = £6,579$$

In order to avoid buying a property at a price where there is a bubble element to it, it's important to know why the bubble element exists and what you need to be aware of to ensure that you never buy a property that is overpriced.

Why the bubble element exists

The bubble element exists due to the following:

Factor	Why
Self-certified borrowing	In the UK we borrow at the current variable base rate and not at the long-term average rate. Currently the long-term rate is around 5.7 per cent and the variable base rate is at four per cent. This is why we have a boom-bust cycle. When rates fall below the long-term rate first-time buyers overborrow, as they can afford it, by obtaining a self-certified mortgage which increases their buying power. Their increase in buying power creates the bubble element as their buying power takes them over the real value of the property.

Factor	Why
Novice investors	Due to the buy-to-let mortgage also operating under the current variable base rate, the same problem occurs. Instead of demanding a two per cent loading over the long-term rate, novice investors demand a two per cent loading over the current variable base rate. This means that you get them buying at six per cent yields and below (if the variable rate is four per cent or below) which supersedes the first-time buyer's highest price.
High-income multiple lending	Some lenders are offering in excess of four times the buyer's salary. This enables a first-time buyer to borrow in excess of the real value of the property, thus creating a bubble element.
Speculative investors	Due to the poor performance of the stock market in recent years, the property market has attracted the traditional stock market investor. Here the investor will invest for capital growth and so will be happy to take less than a two per cent loading. The speculative investor will make the estimation that the growth experienced in the past will happen in the future over the short term. The speculative investor's bid then supersedes the property investor's bid and if this is in excess of a first-time buyer's bid, then a bubble element will exist.
Consumer debt	Some people borrow the deposit for a property by way of a loan. This means that they can enter the property market very quickly as they don't have to wait to save up for a deposit. This increases the number of buyers, thus increasing the demand for property, which pushes up the price of the property.

Assumptions

I have made several assumptions in this calculation which I welcome you to challenge. I have made them in order to make the theory simple, but property investing is not an exact science. Understanding that assumptions can be wrong will help you get beneath the theory and allow you to take a practical approach when making an investment decision. My assumptions that need to be challenged are as follows:

Assumption	Why
95 per cent of advertised price as current market value of property	This is an approximation in a rising market. It may be 100 per cent or even 105 per cent for a competitive market. Use your own experience to decide for yourself how the market is.
Two per cent loading for investor on government gilt rate	It could be more than two per cent. I expect a 6.5 per cent loading for my investments resulting in a 12 per cent plus yield requirement, but I reckon it bottoms out to two per cent loading (because in order to take the risk the lowest compensatory return is two per cent above the risk-free rate equating to 7.62 per cent). However, I may be wrong!
Four times salary lending	This is currently what most lenders offer, but there are lenders that offer up to five times the buyer's salary. If this type of lending grows, the real value of property will rise.
First-time buyer having only five per cent deposit	You can buy a property with no deposit. 100 per cent mortgages are popular, but they don't form a significant part of the market. However, they may do so in the future.
Including only first-time-buyer properties	I've assumed that first-time-buyer properties are the type of properties that investors go for. This isn't a hard and fast rule. Some landlords invest in executive detached properties with lower yields and class A1 tenants. You need to incorporate this into your thinking.

Awareness table

Based on my theory above, we can narrow down what we should be aware of if we really want to understand and exploit property price movements:

Aware of	Description
Global rates	Our rates are restricted by global rates. We cannot be out of sync with the rest of the world. This is called 'interest rate parity'. The formula is as follows: $$\frac{F}{S} = \left(\frac{1 + R^A}{1 + R^B} \right)^T$$ Here, S is the spot exchange rate, expressed as the price in currency A of one unit of currency B; F is the forward rate; R^A and R^B are the interest rates in the respective countries; and T is the common maturity for the forward rate and the two interest rates. This formula assumes that if interest rates are ten per cent in Europe, we will go and convert all our sterling to euros, place them on deposit in a European bank and then convert them back after a year and enjoy the profit. This theory states that the profit would be nil due to the fact that when you converted it back to sterling, you would get an inferior exchange rate. Therefore, we are all locked into each country's interest rate. The world has been in a recession. Interest rates have been low in the major economic countries which have kept the UK's rates low, even though we are not in a recession. Once rates start moving upwards over the borders, then our rates will rise. You need to be aware of the financial indicators of the major economic countries. They will be the same as 'home rates' – see below.
Home rates	Taking into account the interest rate parity above, there will still be some freedom within the UK to set rates. The rate is set by the Bank of England and they use the following reports to set them:

Aware of	Description
	• **Consumer Price Index** – This measures price inflation. The target for the bank is 2.5 per cent. If it goes over, then the Bank is expected to put the rates up. • **Employment Cost Index** – This measures the growth of wages. If wages rise above expectations, this causes an increase in spending which results in inflation. Consequently, the Bank is expected to put the rates up. • **GDP (Gross Domestic Product) Report** – This measures the overall performance of our economy. If it falls two quarters in a row, then we are in a recession and the Bank is expected to lower the rates. • **Unemployment Rate** – This measures the number of people out of work. If it is too low, it causes an increase in spending which results in inflation. Consequently, the Bank is expected to put the rates up. • **House Price Inflation** – This is very underrated by the Bank! I don't know what threshold it sets here, but it is willing to see massive inflation in this area and do nothing about it. However, be aware that the Bank does consider house price inflation when setting rates. Keep abreast, where possible, of the UK and global reports surrounding each country's economy. Here you'll be able to see the triggers to movements in the UK and global interest base rates.
20-year government gilt figure	By knowing this figure you can calculate the real value of the property as the real value is dependent on a two per cent loading of this rate.
Differential between long-term rate and current rate	If there's a significant difference between the long-term rate and the current rate, then the property prices can be abnormally more or less than their real property value. At the moment there's nothing to worry about and the differential is reducing.

Aware of	Description
	However, close inspection of the differential will keep you ahead of the pack as you will see how the lenders react and how property prices change. Also, be aware of heavily discounted mortgage products coming into the market. These deals can distort prices if they become popular as they force other lenders to reduce their rates, making the whole mortgage market even more competitive than it already is!
Rental value of property	For you to really exploit all the possible opportunities, you need to be aware of the rental values of property. Based on this, you can calculate the real value of a property in conjunction with your required return, which you can then compare to the actual asking price. If the real value is in excess of the asking price, then take a look at the property!
Current market value of property	For you to really exploit all the possible opportunities, you need to be aware of the current market value of property. This involves searching on the Internet, looking in local papers and talking to estate agents. Based on your real value of property calculations you can see if the current market value looks attractive.
Negative equity	If there are a significant number of property owners in negative equity, this reduces the feel-good factor. In turn, it reduces spending and productivity. This can trigger a recession which results in higher unemployment and a fall in property prices.
Ratio of earnings to property value	If property values are in excess of four times the buyer's salary, then you know that there is a bubble element to the property price. Try to get local data on people's earnings to help you determine the real price of the property.
Lending multiples	Check to see if lending multiples are increasing. Currently the standard is four, but there are a

Aware of	Description
	growing number of lenders offering 4.25 times the buyer's salary, which is causing the real price of property to rise.
Number of first-time buyers	There needs to be a healthy number to keep the market buoyant, especially where the investors have refused to invest. If first-time buyers stop buying in an area, then prices will fall to the price that an investor would buy at.

Are we heading for a crash?

Will the bubble burst? The short answer is no. This is because the size of the bubble is small and will only burst for a small section of people. Let me explain.

There are only three parties involved within property who can cause a crash:

1. The lender

2. The investor

3. The first-time buyer

The lender

The lender can cause a crash by overlending. All lenders set parameters for lending criteria. Their key lending criteria is four times the buyer's salary for owner-occupiers and 130 per cent of the mortgage payment for buy-to-let investors. Based on these parameters, mortgages should never become unaffordable. This will only happen if the interest rates rise sharply or we enter into a recession. As the lenders are willing to lend, buyers are able to buy and this keeps the market active.

The investor

The investor can cause a crash by miscalculating his returns. If an investor has done his homework, this won't occur as he will never buy over the real price of a property

The first-time buyer

The first-time buyer can cause a crash by overborrowing. Overborrowing requires the first-time buyer to mislead the lender to obtain higher borrowings than he's entitled to. The majority of first-time buyers are unable or unwilling to mislead a lender.

The only people for whom the bubble will burst are the people who hold a property where a bubble exists (see the table on pages 68–9):

- First-time buyers on self-certified borrowing
- Novice investors
- High-income multiple first-time buyers
- Speculative investors
- First-time buyers who have borrowed the deposit

These are a very small section of the market!

Even where bubbles exist the size of the bubbles are small. There will be the professional investor or the standard first-time buyer who will purchase his property off these type of purchasers detailed in the table on pages 68–9 at the real price, which will only be a fraction less than what they paid. In other words, the difference between the inflated price and the real price is very small, therefore no crash should occur.

Outside the property market

The basis of this thinking is that interest rates will not rise beyond affordability and we are not heading for a recession for some time. There can be shocks to the market which no-one can predict, but based on the information we have at hand, it doesn't seem that there will be another crash like the one that occurred in the '90s. This is because we haven't seen the days of 15 per cent base rates in the UK or any of the major unemployment figures of the past for a long time.

CHAPTER 5

Appreciation

Capital appreciation can be amassed by one of three ways:

1. Identifying properties without foresight
2. Identifying properties with foresight
3. Identifying properties with potential

Identifying properties without foresight

Capital appreciation has to be real. Remember the equation:

Pactual = Preal + Pbubble

Real capital appreciation has to be based on the real price, then and now. Anything else is just a bubble! You should sell when a bubble exists as you maximise your exit price (see Chapter 7 for further information on when to exit), but, hopefully, you will see through several bubbles during your time in property investment before you exit.

Despite this, you should still only ever be interested in real capital appreciation during your ownership period. This is because it's real! You know that the real price is the bottom price that you can expect for your property. Bubbles are temporary inflations or deflations of prices which burst back to the real price. They only distort things and are washed out in the long run.

The way to guarantee real capital growth is to buy when there is a negative bubble. I always invest in negative bubble areas as when the bubble bursts prices, instead of falling, rise dramatically.

Look at this example that is based on true events which occurred to me only recently:

I bought some properties in East Yorkshire. One I purchased in Hull was advertised at £29,995 with a rental value of £295. The figures worked out as follows:

Pactual = £29,995 x 95% = **£28,495**

Preal = the higher of:

- what an investor would pay for it: annual rental ÷ (long-term average rate + 2% loading) = (£295 x 12) ÷ (5.62% + 2%) = **£46,457**

- what a first-time buyer would pay for it: (salary of someone willing to live in property x 4) ÷ 0.95 = (£14,000 x 4) ÷ 0.95 = **£58,947**

So the Preal is the higher amount, which is £58,947.

Pbubble = Pactual minus Preal = £28,495 minus £58,947 = **–£30,452**

In this instance I bought a property for £28,495 that is actually worth £58,947 – that's £30,452 locked-in capital growth because it's REAL! So what is it actually worth now? Well, it's worth about £36,000, which is far from its real value of £58,947. However, the negative bubble of £30,452 is exploding. The growth that I have experienced of around £7,500 has occurred in the last three months and the rest will occur over the next year. I know with certainty that the £30,452 will blow up in my face far quicker than the average growth rates for the UK will ever do.

Remember that this certain capital growth is dependent on **both** of the following principles holding:

1. We are not in a recession so there is an abundance of first-time buyers.

2. The buy-to-let market exists so there is an abundance of buy-to-let investors.

Why do negative bubbles exist?

The only real answer to this is that it's because we live in an imperfect market!

There is a limited supply of funds offered to us from the lenders so they have to make a choice whether to lend to:

1. an investor who is unaware of superior markets such as the Hull example and wishes to buy a lower-yielding property in a more conventional and favoured area; OR

2. a private individual who wishes to buy a property in an area that is not considered 'low value'; OR

3. an investor or private individual who wishes to buy in a low-value area.

Usually lenders choose either option 1 or 2 and forget about 3. This is because they think that their money is safer within a property that is valued as more than a 'low-value' property (typically £60,000). This is very short-sighted and, to be honest, it's a stupid view of property lending. However, this is where people like me succeed. There are some lenders, although they're only a handful, who lend on properties of 'low value'. If you buy low down enough, then the only way is up!

Speak to your broker about low-value lenders. If your broker isn't fluent in these type of lenders, then speak to my broker Liz Syms and you will receive a 50 per cent discount on her fees – see Chapter 2 for her details.

Using lenders to your advantage

Now that I've told you how lenders favour higher-value properties, it's time to look at the flipside of the equation. Let's forget low-value areas and look at high-value areas. Consider a flat in Kensington, London. Let's assume that you've done the research and you have found the average salary for the first-time buyer in this area to be £75,000. A one-bedroom property comes up for sale for £250,000, with the rental value at £1,000pcm.

Pactual = £250,000 x 95% = **£237,500**

Preal = the higher of:

- what an investor would pay for it: annual rental ÷ (long-term average rate + 2% loading) = (£1,000 x 12) ÷ (5.62% + 2%) = **£157,480**

- what a first-time buyer would pay for it: (salary of someone willing to live in property x 4) ÷ 0.95 = (£75,000 x 4) ÷ 0.95 = **£315,789**

So the Preal is the higher amount, which is £315,789.

Pbubble = Pactual minus Preal = £237,500 minus £315,789 = **–£78,289**

The negative bubble is £78,289. As I mentioned previously, this certain capital growth is dependent on the holding of both of the principles mentioned on page 78.

However, in this instance, certain capital growth will only occur if there is an abundance of first-time buyers. This is because the buy-to-let investor is not interested, so your only market is the owner-occupier who is willing to pay the price of £315,789. This is what I call the speculative market. You are basically aiming to sell to the owner-occupier, which can be a fickle market. However, if you get it right, then you can make massive gains.

Property programmes, such as *Property Ladder*, have fuelled this type of investment of selling to the private individual. However, please, please, please understand that this is not the basis of property investment. These programmes are only being made credible due to rocketing prices (or negative bubbles bursting – depending on your point of view!)

Look at the disparity of the numbers:

What an investor would pay	£157,480
What an owner-occupier would pay	£315,789
Difference	**£158,309**

So when or if the owner-occupier market collapses, you're left with a property that you thought you could sell for £315,789 but it's actually worth, in real terms, £157,480. This is why trying to sell to the owner-occupier market is high risk.

Identifying properties with foresight

OK, so you want to be clever! If you don't want to make money the easy way by identifying the properties available that will lock in certain growth, then let's play the speculative market. Property prices will rise, in real terms, due to an increased demand for:

- unique properties that are scarce, such as riverside apartments or three-bedroom properties, where there's a glut of two-bedroom properties or houses in central districts as opposed to flats;

- properties that are considered 'safe' and more profitable investments to overseas investors compared to what's available back home;

- an area that has increased in desirability due to major employers locating in the area, improved transport links, such as an addition of a train station, tube or carriageway, or improved services to an area such as a good school, leisure facilities or a shopping centre;

- properties that are next to an area that's booming which makes the area in question highly desirable as it's cheaper than the booming area even after travel and time costs;

- properties that are brand new, with a qualitative effect being produced due to new properties being most sought after;

- an area undergoing a regeneration programme resulting in a general uplift in the area.

This type of speculative investment is less certain. This is because you are:

1. not in possession of all the information; or

2. asking the prospective purchaser of your property what all these extras are worth. (Even if you're not selling the property, these extras will ultimately determine its real value.)

The reason why it's difficult to quantify these extras is because they are qualitative as well as quantitative. What is the true worth of a property next to a train station compared to a property ten minutes away from the station? Is it £5,000 or £50,000? This, of course, determines the average selling price.

Take, for example, a riverside apartment on the north side of the river in London. How many properties are there for sale? Let's say that there are ten properties. Out of those, how many need to be sold? The answer is very few. How many people are actively looking for a north-side riverside apartment? Loads! So for scarce, highly-desirable properties, it's a seller's market. This means that you simply have to wait for the buyer to come along unless you are forced to sell. The only reason you may be forced to sell is if you need the proceeds to buy your next place or interest rates are on the up to the point that you can't afford the mortgage payments.

If you have a desired property, you can wait for the buyer to come to you **and** achieve the price you want as long as you can hold out for a buyer.

Having a desired property like those listed above will incorporate a qualitative factor within the price. Current thinking says that there is no way to quantify these qualitative factors, hence you can receive ridiculous amounts for seemingly basic extras such as being next door to a tube station, offering a brand new property or being next to a booming area as it's highly desired.

One thing I am noticing in the market these days is the increased value of time. There is a real perceived value in a property that is located in an area that saves you time commuting. A property located one minute closer in travel time can have a disproportionate increase in value if it is measured to the worker's hourly rate. This is because the worker's leisure time is worth more than what he earns. It's worth looking at the properties that are, or potentially, able to save the buyer/tenant over 15 minutes in commuting time.

Identifying properties with potential

This section is for people who like to make money the hard way! You can add value immediately to a property if you are willing to enhance it. You can enhance a property in a number of ways:

1. Refurbish it

2. Extend the property

3. Convert the loft

Refurbish it

A real synergy can be created if you get this right. Synergy means that the sum is greater than its parts or, some people like to say, 2 + 2 = 5. Let me explain.

Joe buys a house for £100,000. He spends £5,000 refurbishing it and sells it immediately for £125,000, thus making:

$$£125,000 \text{ minus } (£100,000 + £5,000) = £20,000$$

So, in this example:

$$£100,000 + £5,000 = £125,000$$

£20,000 has miraculously appeared from nowhere! The reason for this amount appearing is due to:

1. **Joe saving time for the buyer** – If a buyer sees the property for £100,000 and it needs refurbishment, he probably won't be interested in it as he doesn't have the time either to do or to supervise someone else to do the refurbishment.

2. **Joe, and not the buyer, having £5,000 to refurbish it** – Joe is a businessman so he has £5,000 to refurbish the property and the buying power to purchase it. The buyer, however, will probably only have enough for the deposit. On a five per cent deposit of £100,000, a private buyer will need £5,000 to buy the property and £5,000 for the refurbishment, totalling £10,000. If the buyer buys the property after Joe has refurbished it, he will only need five per cent x £125,000 = £6,250. Therefore, the buyer needs less money to purchase the property after refurbishment.

3. **Joe is an expert** – Joe will probably have the contacts, know-how and expertise to refurbish the property cheaper than a private individual as he's in the trade. Therefore, if Joe views the property alongside an amateur investor, Joe will cost the job at £5,000 and the amateur investor may work it out to be £8,000. Due to Joe's ability to price the job lower than the amateur, he can go in with a higher offer than the amateur – well, in theory anyway! After watching programmes like *Property Ladder*, *House Doctor*, etc., everyone now thinks that he is a property developer! As a result, amateur investors are under-budgeting

for the refurbishment and overestimating the eventual selling price, thus pushing the professional investor out.

Now, I'll be honest with you. I know absolutely nothing about the construction or refurbishment of property! I have only refurbished properties when they were so cheap that I couldn't resist them. I once purchased a seven-bedroom property (yes, seven bedrooms!) for £42,000 in Corby. I never saw it, but I heard that it was completely vandalised inside as it was an old crack house. I knew that I could let it out at £500pcm after refurbishment so I considered it to be worth £50,000 at least. If the refurbishment would cost less than £8,000, then purchasing the property made sense. I managed to get a quote for £5,000 and went ahead with the refurbishment!

There are various books published on how to add value to a property by making it look pretty, but this isn't one of them! If you want to play this game, you have to look at the numbers carefully. You need to check that there is a safe profit margin in it for you. So, what is safe? You should always be prudent. In other words, you should always overestimate your costs and underestimate your proceeds. Look at this example:

There is a property for sale for £100,000 that would be worth £150,000 if it was refurbished under the current market conditions. The cost of the refurbishment is estimated at £10,000 and will take two months. I would adopt this forecasted profit and loss:

Selling price: 90%* of anticipated selling price = 90% x £150,000	£135,000
Estate agent's fees: 1% + VAT	(£1,586)
Net proceeds	**£133,414**

* as opposed to 95% presuming that the vendor has overestimated the selling price

Costs:	
Purchase price	£100,000
Refurbishment: 150% x estimated costs	£15,000
Loan repayments: six months' interest (£100,000 x 5% x 6/12)	£2,500
Total costs	(£117,500)
Anticipated profit	**£15,914**

Prudently, it will take you six months to make £15,914, totalling £31,828 per annum. Now is this worth your time and money? For me it isn't, but it may be for you. You'll be surprised how people don't do this simple profit and loss account to really see if a project is worth their time. Remember, also, that it's anticipated profit – it could be more **or** less!

Extend the property

It's **not** a blanket rule that if you extend a property it increases the value of the property over and above what you spent on the extension. It heavily depends on where your property is located. I have created a way of calculating how much your property will increase in price if you splash out on an extension.

It's all to do with the ratio of land to building cost. If you build on desired land, then you win, but if you don't, you lose! So how do we find out if we own a property sitting on desired land? Well, it's all to do with the rebuild cost of your house, which should be stated on your building insurance policy. This would have been determined when you last had the property surveyed.

Now, in order to decide if the land is desired, you simply calculate the following ratio:

$$\frac{\text{Current market value}}{\text{Rebuild cost}}$$

If the ratio is greater than one, then it's desired. If it's less than one, it's not.

For example, if Jack has a property that is currently worth £100,000 and the rebuild cost is £60,000, then the current market value rebuild ratio is:

$$\frac{£100,000}{£60,000} = 1.667$$

which is greater than one. Therefore, Jack should extend his property.

If Jill also has a property worth £100,000 and it has a rebuild cost of £120,000, then the ratio is:

$$\frac{£100,000}{£120,000} = 0.833$$

which is less than one. Therefore, Jill shouldn't extend her property.

You should use this ratio as a multiplier to determine how much value will be added to the property. In the above examples, if they both decided to spend £30,000 on a downstairs extension, then their properties, as a rule of thumb, would increase by:

1.667 x £30,000 = approximately £50,000 for Jack

0.833 x £30,000 = approximately £25,000 for Jill

Here, Jack makes a £20,000 profit (£50,000 minus £30,000) as a result of the extension, whereas Jill makes a £5,000 loss (£25,000 minus £30,000) as a result of hers.

Remember that this is only an approximation. It all depends on how you extend, your choice of materials and whether you add a bedroom or a dining room. There are many books available on what particular things add value to a property and I advise you to read them if you intend to extend. This multiplier should help you decide whether to extend or not. If the multiplier is greater than two and you are willing to take on such a project, then the decision to extend is a no-brainer, i.e. you definitely should!

Convert the loft

It's difficult not to justify such an improvement to a property. They are cheap to do and they can add one of the most powerful increases to a property price – an extra bedroom! In order to calculate whether you should do a conversion, use the multiplier above, but multiply it by three. Let me show you using the same example as above:

Jack's multiplier	1.667 x 3 = 5.00
Jill's multiplier	0.833 x 3 = 2.5

If Jack and Jill both spend £5,000 on a loft conversion, they can expect an uplift in the values of their homes by:

Jack:	5 x £5,000 = £25,000
Jill:	2.5 x £5,000 = £12,500

Jack and Jill can expect to profit from their loft conversion to the tune of £20,000 and £7,500 respectively.

CHAPTER 6

Risk

If you want to earn a greater return than a risk-free rate, such as a building society rate or a government gilt rate, then you have to accept a degree of risk. There is no such thing as a free lunch! Therefore, the risk we are thinking to accept when entering or remaining in the property market has to be:

1. understood;

2. eliminated (where possible); and

3. managed.

I want you to apply this to any business investment, not only to property. The key to long-term business success lies within this chapter. You have to understand the risks involved, eliminate them where possible and manage the risks that remain.

Understanding risk

The following mutually exclusive risks exist in property investment:

Risk	Description
Systematic risk	This is the simple risk of being in the property market.
Leverage risk	This risk is associated with borrowing. If you borrow money to buy a property, then you have to

Risk	Description
	pay it back – with interest! If you default on the repayments, you can be out of business very quickly and be declared bankrupt.
Specific risk	Specific risk is the risk you face with the individual property and tenant. It has nothing to do with the property market or borrowing.

These risks are mutually exclusive as they operate under very different conditions. The property market as a whole is dependent on demographics; the borrowing rates are set largely on global and home economies, and your relationship with your tenant is individual. This means that you can tackle each risk independently. If you manage to eliminate any of the risks, you can then focus on the risks that remain. Here are the following risks that can be eliminated:

Risk	Eliminated?
Systematic risk	Yes
Leverage risk	Yes
Specific risk	No

So you can see that both systematic risk and leverage risk can be eliminated. Specific risk is an individual risk which can be managed – see below for further information.

Eliminating risk

Systematic risk

Systematic risk occurs merely from investing in the property market. However, the property market is here to stay and is therefore less risky compared to a new-product business. With a new product, you have to estimate the market in order to gauge demand, but the property market will always be in demand. As long as you can ride the boom-bust cycles, you will ALWAYS win as property delivers a higher rate of return than the risk-free rate.

Systematic risk is eliminated in the same way as it's eliminated when you are holding a stock portfolio. There will always be the stock market and there will always be businesses to invest in. The key to eliminating systematic risk is to invest in stocks that are uncorrelated, i.e. if one stock was to collapse, it would have no impact on any other stock. This is called diversification. If you have a well-diversified portfolio, then the stocks you hold will have a near-zero correlation with the others.

The way to do this is to invest in uncorrelated markets such as the following:

Uncorrelated Markets	Description
Industry, e.g. pharmaceuticals versus financial services	If you invest in a number of industries that have a low correlation and one industry suffers, it should not affect your holdings in the other industries. In this example, you could probably find a link between drugs and the financial services, but it would be very small. These markets should act independently.
Area, e.g. Asian markets versus Atlantic markets	If you invest in different countries, you can expect a lower correlation between stocks held in each individual country than if you invested in individual stocks within the same country. Now we all know the saying 'if the US sneezes, we all catch a cold', but in this example the Asian market does have its own economy, which largely functions on its own independent variables. If an Asian crash did occur, it should not largely affect your holding in the US.
Type, e.g. stocks versus bonds	The bond market operates on different fundamentals to the stock market so there is a low correlation between the two. A well-diversified portfolio will have a mixture of stocks and bonds.

So how does this transfer to the property market? You have to look at the markets within the property market and ensure that your portfolio is well diversified, i.e. that your property portfolio is spread among several uncorrelated markets.

When I say uncorrelated I mean significantly, but not absolutely. Nothing is 100 per cent uncorrelated. You can always find a link to something no matter how unrelated the two markets appear to be. The term uncorrelated is used in a broad sense. The broad uncorrelated markets that exist within the property market are:

Markets	Uncorrelated Markets	Description
Industry	Private versus DSS tenant	The DSS market will largely depend on the local council's ability to operate efficiently and pay market rents. The private market will depend on employment rates and rates of pay. These are independent, hence they are uncorrelated.
	Single versus family tenant	The single-person market is fuelled by the property's proximity to bars, restaurants and gyms, etc. and a high tenant turnover is expected. The family tenant is more concerned with the proximity to schools, parks and leisure facilities. The single-person let and the family let operate under different conditions, hence they are uncorrelated.
Area	Area 1 versus area 2	Significant uncorrelation exists between regions, i.e. the South East, the South West, East Anglia, London, East Midlands, West Midlands, the West, Wales, the North West, the North East, Scotland and Northern Ireland. They operate to their own fundamentals.

Markets	Uncorrelated Markets	Description
	UK versus overseas	Significant uncorrelation exists between countries. They operate to their own fundamentals.
Type	Private versus ex-local-authority or low-value homes	It's quite normal to see the prices of low-value homes boom and the executive developments fall or vice versa at the same time. These markets act independently as the purchasers or tenants for each of these types of properties lead very different lives and have different jobs. If executive jobs are reducing but manual work is increasing, then this will happen.

To have a well-diversified portfolio which eliminates systematic risk, you will need a fair mix across the portfolio of the following:

- Private and DSS tenants
- Single tenants and family tenants
- Properties located in all regions of the UK
- Properties located around the world
- Private properties and low-value ex-local-authority properties

Now, I can already hear you saying, 'Yeah, great, but I'm not a billionaire who can buy every type of property in every region in the UK and every country in the world!' This is true, but this portfolio is an ideal which you should always aim for, even if you never reach it.

Leverage risk

So let's assume that you are not a billionaire, but you want to aim for a well-diversified portfolio. If you want to achieve it quickly, you will have to borrow in order to buy a number of properties in differing markets. This then introduces leverage risk, which is the risk that you will overborrow, end up defaulting on your loan repayments and eventually go bankrupt.

The way to eliminate leverage risk is to acquire a well-diversified portfolio immediately or over time without borrowing. You won't grow as fast as an investor willing to accept leverage risk, but once it has been achieved you will be sitting on a major cash-generating machine. This method is really only suitable for people who are the following:

- **Of high net worth** – They have large reserves of cash at hand or have recently liquidised their poor performing property or stock portfolio and wish to buy a superior property portfolio for cash.

- **Not relying on a property portfolio** – They have a high income already which they can live on and their income is also high enough that they can save and buy a property for cash.

- **In receipt of a large inheritance or cash windfall** – They have come into a significant amount of money and intend to earn a rate in excess of the risk-free rate (e.g. a building society savings account).

- **Managing a significant investment fund** – They are in the privileged position of managing other people's money collectively and may not need to borrow to achieve full diversification as the fund will be large enough to spread around a large number of properties.

If you are not in any of the fortunate positions above, then the bad news is that you will have to accept leverage risk. The good news is that it can be managed along with specific risk.

Managing risk

Leverage risk

Let me remind you of what leverage risk is:

The risk that you will overborrow, end up defaulting on your loan repayments and eventually go bankrupt.

This is the main reason why businesses go under. Even the big boys can get it wrong, for example, Worldcom and Swiss Air, who wouldn't have gone bankrupt if they had managed their debt appropriately.

To manage your debt you need to **act** prior to taking on new debt and **react** to the changing conditions during the term of the debt. The risks you face from debt and the actions and reactions you can do are as follows:

Risk	Action	Reaction
The loan amount is too big to pay in full and on time	• **Do your homework!** You must budget for what you can afford. Be sure to factor in the tenant not paying or unexpected repair bills. • **Borrow less** – You don't need to gear up to 85 per cent LTV if the figures don't stack up. If you can finance the purchase with only 60 per cent LTV borrowing, do so.	• **Reduce the loan amount** – If you have any money in a savings account that can ease your problem, then use it to redeem some of the debt. • **Refinance** – You may be able to refinance the debt by switching to lenders offering a better rate or increasing the term of the debt. • **Sell** – If you can't do any of the above, then get out before it gets you!
Interest rates rise making the loan repayment too big to pay infull and on time	• **Fix your interest rates** – This is a common way to manage an interest rate rise risk. • **Spread your borrowing over different lenders** – Lenders have different rates and adjust to an interest rate rise differently.	• **Reduce the loan amount** – If you have any money in a savings account that could ease your problem, use it to redeem some of the debt. • **Refinance** – You may be able to refinance the debt by switching to lenders offering a better rate or

Risk	Action	Reaction
	• **Borrow less** – You don't need to gear up to 85 per cent LTV if the figures don't stack up. If you can finance the purchase with only 60 per cent LTV borrowing, then do so.	increasing the term of the debt. • **Sell** – If you can't do any of the above, get out before it gets you!

Now we know how to manage leverage risk, let's discuss the details of managing specific risk associated with each individual property.

Specific risk

The way to mitigate against the risks involved in investing in property, hence managing them, is to take countermeasure actions. There are five specific risks that can happen to an individual investment property and the corresponding countermeasure actions you can take to manage these risks are:

Risk	Countermeasure
Can't find a tenant	• Buy a property that can be easily let out (e.g. property near a major train station or in a desirable area). • Reduce the rent.
Getting caught in a negative equity trap	• Don't sell the property and realise your loss. Continue to rent it out. Wait for the recovery and then sell it. • Buy the property without a mortgage so that negative equity is not a possibility.
The tenant doesn't pay the rent	• Take out landlord insurance that covers you for loss of rent due to the tenant defaulting.

Risk	Countermeasure
Major repairs are due and you can't afford to carry out the work	• Take out a thorough and comprehensive building and contents insurance. • Take out specific policies for specific items, e.g. British Gas offer full insurance on your boiler from £8 per month.
Buying a property you can't sell	• Avoid properties that are difficult to sell, such as studio flats, ex-local-authority flats, flats above shops, non-standard construction properties or any property that is difficult to get a mortgage on. • Buy a property near a train station, city or major road junction.

Overall risk

Knowing, understanding and addressing all the risks you face in business is a hot topic. Risk and business go hand in hand so it's fundamental to grasp the whole notion of risk if you want to take business seriously.

You should examine your overall exposure to risk and see how well you are managing these risks. Remember, you can always do something to lower your overall risk. This chapter only touches on risk management. There is a whole science out there that's worthy of a read. Simply search for 'risk management' on www.google.co.uk and you'll find a whole number of tools to identify and control all the risks being faced by a business.

CHAPTER 7

Exit

It's all about going out on a high! They always say to leave on a high note and this also includes property investment – except you leave on a high price!

To know when to sell you have to understand, what I call, the property quadrant.

The property quadrant

Look at this quadrant:

4 + YIELD & – GROWTH (WARMSPOT)	+ YIELD & + GROWTH (HOTSPOT) 1
– YIELD & – GROWTH (COLDSPOT) 3	– YIELD & + GROWTH (COOLING SPOT) 2

Negative and positive yield growths can be defined as:

Term	Definition
+/– yield	A positive yield means that, as a result of your investment, cash is put into your pocket. ALL expenses are taken into account, which includes interest payments, void periods, repairs, management fees and tax.

Term	Definition
	A negative yield means that, as a result of your investment, cash is taken out of your pocket. This is due to increased interest payments (caused by an increase in interest rates or overborrowing), higher voids (caused by over-supply of the rental market) and large repair bills.
+/– growth	A positive growth means that the property's value is on an upward trend.
	A negative growth means that the property's value is on a downward trend.

The definitions of a hotspot, cooling spot, coldspot and warmspot and the type of buyers for properties located in these areas are:

1. + YIELD & + GROWTH (HOTSPOT)

Description

Since we are in a rising property price market overall, you should only ever invest in this place. This investment puts money in your pocket and it also enables you to grow quickly because you can access the capital growth by remortgaging. As prices rise (due to the professional investors competing for the same properties) the yields fall until they go negative. Then the hotspot goes to a cooling spot – see below.

Typical Region: The North

Buyers: Professional investors, owner-occupiers

2. – YIELD & + GROWTH (COOLING SPOT)

Description

This is where even though the investment takes cash out of your pocket, investors are banking on capital gain to give them a return. This situation can only last until their money runs out. At some point they have to sell, which causes the market to become a buyer's market rather than a seller's market and prices fall, creating negative growth. It then becomes a coldspot – see below.

Typical Region: London

Buyers: Bandwagon investors, amateur investors, owner-occupiers

3. – YIELD & – GROWTH (COLDSPOT)

Description

No-one wants these properties as investments! These investments are bad for your wealth. The only buyers are owner-occupiers who want to live in the property rather than rent it out. When owner-occupiers are unable to buy due to unaffordability a rapid decline occurs. Certain areas will become warmspots – see below.

Typical Region: Posh areas (e.g. Kensington, Cambridge and Oxford)

Buyers: No investors as it is negative yield AND negative growth. Owner-occupiers only.

4. + YIELD & – GROWTH (WARMSPOT)

Description

While rapidly declining, certain areas will still put cash in your pocket, even though they continue to decline. Considering the market is only heading downwards, only professional investors will take the chance as the investment is cash positive. Owner-occupiers will wait for the market to bottom out. Property prices will recover due to rental price increases, falling interest rates and properties becoming affordable. Hence a warmspot becomes a hotspot – see above.

Typical Region: None currently

Buyers: Professional investors in a falling market. The professionals see that these investments are better than leaving their cash in the bank. No owner-occupiers.

There's no point in selling your property when it's in a hotspot (unless you want to sell your portfolio in one hit – see below). This is because there's still room for the price to grow and it's currently profitable so it's not costing you to own it. It only becomes worth selling when the property becomes unprofitable, but the price is still growing. The highest point in the market can only ever exist within a cooling spot. This is because the property price has risen to the point that it's unprofitable, but it's still on an upward trend. The professional investor drops out of buying in this market and only owner-occupiers and novice investors remain.

You will be able to sell within this market as there are owner-occupiers who are not concerned about the profitability of a property as they wish to live in it rather than rent it out. There are also speculative investors out there who are banking on the continuing increase of property prices and the novice investor not doing his sums right. The reasons why these buyers are able to buy your property at an inflated price above the real price are outlined in the table on pages 68–9.

It's these type of buyers who cause the bubble in the property market – so use them to your advantage!

Selling the portfolio in one hit

If you want to sell your portfolio as one job lot, you have no choice but to sell to the dreaded 'professional investor'! He will look beyond whether the tenant pays the rent on time, a tenancy exists or the décor is up to date. Instead, he wants to know the core fundamentals.

A professional investor will only ever invest in warm- or hotspots. Since various hotspots exist, he will only invest in a warmspot for non-financial reasons. This may be due to the fact that he lives near the warmspot, has knowledge of the area or has a preference not to invest in a hotspot due to the type of tenant.

You should preferably position your property portfolio for sale when it is in a hotspot. At least the property portfolio value is growing and the professional investor may over-speculate and give you that little bit more, banking on further rises, which are probably likely. You should avoid selling in a warmspot as the value of the property portfolio is falling and the professional investor will use this to his advantage and over-discount his offer to you.

One thing to learn in all this is never, never, never sell in a coldspot. This is where the general property market loses but the professional investor survives as he never realises his losses. Selling in a falling market can cost you dearly.

The professional investor will want to know the following:

- The individual price wanted for each property
- The individual yield information on each property

- The overall yield on the whole portfolio

- The Profit & Loss Account for the portfolio

- The types of tenancies existing on all the properties

- Anything unique to any of the properties, such as flying freeholds (properties that sit above land that isn't owned, e.g. a flat on a bridge), etc.

Capital Gains Tax

This tax only arises when you sell the property. The capital gain is worked out as:

Sale price minus purchase price = capital gain

The sale price is deemed to be the price achieved after deducting estate agent's costs, solicitor's fees and any other expenses that were incurred wholly, necessarily and exclusively in the sale of the property.

The purchase price is the cost of the property plus all survey and legal costs.

How to reduce your capital gain

The calculation

The way to reduce your capital gain is to understand the capital gain calculation. If you dispose of a property, the following calculation will be made to work out your capital gain:

	Sale price		£125,000
minus	Allowable costs		£100,000
	Purchase price	£80,000	
	Incidental costs of purchase	£2,000	
	Home improvements	£15,000	

	Costs of establishing or defending title	£1,000
	Selling costs	£2,000
=	Chargeable gain	**£25,000**

The sale price and the purchase price are fixed. You cannot change what you sold the property for or what you paid for it.

Allowable costs

To reduce your capital gain, you have to maximise the other allowable costs. Let's look at these and what you can include. This part is paraphrased from the Inland Revenue themselves:

Allowable Costs	What You Can Include
Incidental costs of purchase	• Fees, commission or remuneration paid for professional advice. • The costs of transferring the property. • Stamp duty. • The costs of advertising to find a seller. • The costs of any valuations needed to work out your chargeable gain (but not the costs of resolving any disagreement with the Inland Revenue about your valuations).
Home improvements	These are costs which: • you incurred for the purpose of enhancing the value of the property; and • are still reflected in the state or nature of the property at the date of its disposal. You may not claim for the cost of normal maintenance and repairs.
Costs of establishing or defending the title	• Fees, commission or remuneration paid for professional advice.

Allowable Costs	What You Can Include
Selling costs	• Fees, commission or remuneration paid for professional advice. • The costs of transferring the property. • The costs of advertising to find a buyer. • The costs of any valuations needed to work out your chargeable gain (but not the costs of resolving any disagreement with the Inland Revenue about your valuations).

Source: Inland Revenue

So in a nutshell you can include:

- Solicitor's costs

- Accountant's fees

- Mortgage broker's fees

- Redemption penalties on cleared mortgages

- Stamp duty

- Advertising

- Estate agent's fees

- Valuations needed to calculate your gain

- Any improvements that still remain in the property

- Legal costs in defending your title to the property

So the first part of reducing your capital gain is to include **all** costs involved with the purchase, ownership period and sale of the property that fall within the definitions stated by the Inland Revenue. Yet it doesn't stop here! You can obtain further relief on the gain:

Taper relief

You can reduce your calculated gain by up to 40 per cent. Take a look at this table:

Number of Whole Years the Property Has Been Owned	Gain Remaining Chargeable (%)
Less than 1	100
1	100
2	100
3	95
4	90
5	85
6	80
7	75
8	70
9	65
10 or more	60

The longer you have owned the property, the less gain you have to pay. In reference to the above table, after three complete years of ownership you start to attract taper relief. After ten years or more, you attract the maximum amount of relief where only 60 per cent of the gain is chargeable or, in other words, a 40 per cent discount on the gain is chargeable.

Please note that it has to be complete years. Another way to reduce your capital gain is to stall your purchase, if possible, to capture another year. Look at this example:

Harry has found a buyer for his investment property that he has owned for five years, 11 months. The capital gain on the sale is £100,000. If he sells straight away, 85 per cent of the gain is chargeable as he is deemed to have owned the asset for five complete years, equating to £85,000. However, if he stalls the sale one month later then he is deemed to have owned the asset for six complete years so only 80 per cent of the gain is chargeable, equating to £80,000. This method only works for the sale of assets that have been owned for two to nine years. Otherwise, it makes no difference.

Personal allowance

You can reduce your gain even further. Everybody gets a Capital Gains Tax allowance of £8,200 (2004–5) per tax year rising year on year with inflation. So if you have a gain of £10,000, it is reduced by £8,200 to £1,800.

If you are selling a couple of properties, the best plan is to sell one before 5 April and one after so, for example, you can use the capital gains allowance for the tax year 2003–4 as well as the one for 2004–5. This then makes full use of your yearly allowances.

There is one final trick – your principal place of residence:

Principal Place of Residence (PPR)

You do not have to pay any Capital Gains Tax on your personal residence. If you move out of home and let it out, and then sell your original residence within three years of leaving, there is no tax to pay! If you sell after the three years, say five years later, you still get relief for three years out of the total five, even if you have purchased another property. Let's look at this example:

Jamie lives in a house that has been his personal residence for eight years when he bought it, but he decides to move out and rent it out. If he sells the property two years after he rented it out, there is no tax to pay. If he sells it five years later then only:

$$\frac{(5 \text{ minus } 3)}{13} \quad \text{of the gain is chargeable.}$$

The equation being:

$$\frac{(\text{Amount of years rented minus three years})}{\text{Period of ownership}}$$

SIPP and FURBS

You may have heard these terms flying about in connection with properties and pensions. Let me explain their relevance to this subject.

SIPP

This stands for Self-Invested Personal Pension. The reason why it is mentioned is that you can buy commercial property within this pension and enjoy all the tax breaks a normal pension has. The reason why a SIPP is not applicable in this situation is because we are investing in residential property. Residential property is not allowed under the SIPP scheme.

Commercial property is not as attractive as residential property, the reasons being that:

- the yields are lower;

- borrowing is restricted to 70 per cent LTV;

- the business risk is doubled as you are reliant on your tenant's business to trade well out of your property, plus there are the normal risks associated with owning the commercial property itself.

This is my own personal opinion. You may think that commercial property is for you. If you do get into this game, I would seriously consider investing in commercial property under the umbrella of a SIPP as the shelter to tax is quite significant.

FURBS

This stands for a Funded Unapproved Retirement Benefit Scheme. Its main beneficiaries are the higher-rate taxpayers only, so if you're not a higher-rate taxpayer and don't expect to be one, ignore this bit.

If you buy a residential property under this umbrella, then:

- profits from the scheme are taxed at 22 per cent rather than 40 per cent if you are a higher-rate taxpayer;

- Capital Gains Tax is 34 per cent in comparison to 40 per cent. A FURBS also attracts the normal taper relief explained above;

- you can pass a FURBS down to your family. There is no Inheritance Tax to pay when it is passed on after death, as opposed to the normal Inheritance Tax limits (currently £263,000 – 2004–5). Also, a traditional pension fund cannot be passed down;

- there is no limit on the contributions to a FURBS, but you don't get any tax relief on your contributions;

- the whole of the fund can be withdrawn tax free compared to a traditional pension fund, which is restricted to 25 per cent;

- you can retire after the age of 75. Traditional pension funds are restricted to an age limit of 75.

The two key things you need to consider when deciding on whether to invest in property using a FURBS are as follows:

1. You can only access the money at retirement, so you can only use the money to make further investments but no money can be taken out to be spent personally. If you want to retire prior to normal retirement age, then it's not possible under this scheme. FURBS restricts your freedom.

2. There are administrational costs involved. You have to use an accountant and the accounting for such a scheme has to be spot on.

Personally, I like the freedom that I have. Maybe when I'm over 45 and FURBS are still about, then I'll consider one. I think that if your target earning is more than £50,000pa profit from property, you presently don't require more than £50,000pa to live on and you're aged over 45, then a FURBS may be for you. Do seek professional advice.

And finally...

Once you've sold up you can buy that yacht that you've always wanted and retire to the South of France, but I suspect you'll be back in a year looking to buy and build up a portfolio again...

Appendix

Useful addresses

Association of Chartered Certified Accountants (ACCA)

64 Finnieston Square	Tel: 0141 582 2000
Glasgow G3 8DT	Email: info@accaglobal.com
	Web: www.acca.co.uk

Association of Residential Lettings Agents (ARLA)

Maple House	Tel: 0845 345 5752
53–55 Woodside Road	Email: info@arla.co.uk
Amersham	Web: www.arla. co.uk
Bucks HP6 6AA	

Association of Residential Managing Agents (ARMA)

178 Battersea Park Road	Tel: 020 7978 2607
London SW11 4ND	Email: info@arma.org.uk
	Web: www.arma.org.uk

Council for Registered Gas Installers (CORGI)

1 Elmwood, Chineham Park	Tel: 0870 401 2300
Crockford Lane	Email: enquiries@corgi-gas.com
Basingstoke	Web: www.corgi-gas-safety.com
Hants RG24 8WG	

Institute of Chartered Accountants in England & Wales (ICAEW)

Chartered Accountants' Hall	Tel: 020 7920 8100
PO Box 433	Web: www.icaew.co.uk
London EC2P 2BJ	

Institute of Plumbing and Heating Engineering (IPHE)

64 Station Lane	Tel: 01708 472 791
Hornchurch	Email: info@iphe.org.uk
Essex RM12 6NB	Web: www.iphe.org.uk

Leasehold Advisory Group (LAG)

Web: www.leaseholdadvice.co.uk

LAG's financial advisors:

Cranfield Asset Management Ltd	Tel: 020 7404 5955
3rd Floor, 9 Staple Inn	
London WC1V 7QH	

LAG's solicitors:

Rooks Rider Solicitors	Tel: 020 7689 7000
Challoner House	Web: www.rooksrider.co.uk
19 Clerkenwell Close	
London EC1R 0RR	

LAG's valuers:

Michael Tims and Company	Tel: 020 7409 2233
80 Duke Street	Web: www.michaeltims.co.uk
Mayfair	
London W1K 6JG	

Leasehold Advisory Service (LEASE)

70–74 City Road	Tel: 0845 345 1993
London EC1Y 2BJ	Email: info@lease-advice.org
	Web: www.lease-advice.org.uk

National Federation of Builders (NFB)

National Office	Tel: 0870 898 9091
55 Tufton Street	Web: www.builders.org.uk
London SW1P 3QL	

National Inspection Council for Electrical Installation Contracting (NICEIC)

Vintage House	Tel: 020 7564 2323
37 Albert Embankment	Email: enquiries@niceic.org.uk
London SE1 7UJ	Web: www.niceic.org.uk

Index

MORE BOOKS AVAILABLE FROM LAWPACK

Separation & Divorce

Separation and divorce do not have to be very costly and difficult. This guide gives you the instructions and information you need to manage your own divorce, without the expense of a solicitor. It explains the legal and financial issues involved, and takes you step-by-step from the petition to the final decree. For use in England & Wales.

Code B445 | ISBN 1 904053 32 7 | Paperback | 240 x 167mm | 224pp | £11.99 | 1st edition

Wills, Power of Attorney & Probate

This guide combines three closely related areas of law; the common theme is the management of personal property and legal affairs. In a Will, you set out whom is to inherit your 'estate'; a power of attorney authorises another to act on your behalf with full legal authority; and via probate (or 'Confirmation' in Scotland), executors gain authority to administer your Will.

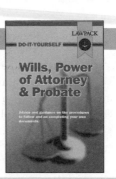

Code B407 | ISBN 1 904053 33 5 | Paperback | 234 x 153mm | 248pp | £11.99 | 1st edition

The Buy-to-Let Bible

Low mortgage rates and under-performance by traditional savings and investment products means that property has never looked a better way to invest for the future. Author Ajay Ahuja divulges the practical and financial techniques that have made him a millionaire. It covers finding the right property, the right mortgage lender, the right tenant, legal issues and tax.

Code B437 | ISBN 1 904053 36 X | Paperback | 234 x 153mm | 256pp | £11.99 | 2nd edition

To order, visit **www.lawpack.co.uk** or call **020 7394 4040**

MORE BOOKS AVAILABLE FROM LAWPACK

Buying Bargains at Property Auctions

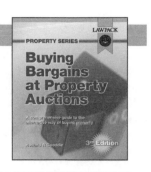

Every week, hundreds of commercial and residential properties are sold at auction in Britain, often at bargain prices, with owner-occupiers accounting for a growing proportion of buyers. In this bestselling guide, author and property auctioneer Howard Gooddie spells out how straightforward the auction route can be and divulges the tips and practices of this relatively unknown world.

Code B426 | ISBN 1 904053 64 5 | Paperback | 250 x 199mm | 176pp | £11.99 | 3rd edition

House Buying, Selling and Conveyancing

It isn't true that only those who have gone through long, expensive and involved training can possibly understand the intricacies of house buying, selling and conveyancing. This best-selling book explains just how straightforward the whole process really is. Required reading for all house buyers (or sellers).

Code B412 | ISBN 1 904053 61 0 | Paperback | 250 x 199mm | 160pp | £11.99 | 4th edition

Residential Lettings

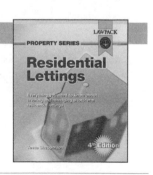

Are you thinking of letting a flat or a house? This guide steers anyone who intends – or already is – letting property through the legal and practical issues involved. It provides all the up-to-date information and tips that a would-be landlord needs. It will also alert existing landlords to the points of good practice that make a letting successful, and the legal obligations that they may not be aware of.

Code B422 | ISBN 1 904053 63 7 | Paperback | 250 x 199mm | 112pp | £11.99 | 4th edition

To order, visit **www.lawpack.co.uk** or call **020 7394 4040**